SUPERIOR SEASONS
life on a northern coast

SUPERIOR SEASONS
life on a northern coast

Shawn Perich

Illustrated by Bob Cary
Cover photo by Gary Alan Nelson

NORTH SHORE PRESS
HOVLAND, MINNESOTA

North Shore Press
5188 North Road
Hovland, MN 55606
(218) 475-2515
www.northshorepress.com

Library of Congress Control Number: 2004090988

ISBN 0-9740207-0-2

Printed in the United States of America by Bang Printing

10 9 8 7 6 5 4 3 2 1

To all the people
with whom I've shared
this wonderful place
we call the North Shore.

Acknowledgements

Most of the stories in this book originally appeared in Minnesota Outdoor News and are reprinted with permission. I am particularly thankful to Outdoor News publisher Glenn Meyer, who gave me the opportunity to write a weekly column with the open-ended direction that it be "about the outdoors." The venerable Cook County News-Herald in Grand Marais, Minnesota deserves a thank-you as well, for publishing my work, including some of these stories, over the last 15 years.

No man, nor writer, is an island. Thanks to Tom Dickson for selecting the stories that appear in this book; to Bob Cary for his classic illustrations; to Amber Pratt and Joy Dey for their design skills; to Ann Possis for her keen proofreading; to Mike Furtman and Susan Gustafson for sound advice; and to my family and friends for encouragement and support. A special thanks is in order for Rob Dreislein, the editor of Outdoor News—and one of the best in the business.

TABLE OF CONTENTS

TABLE OF CONTENTS

Out in the Popples

Deer Season

Settling In

Foreword

You can accumulate lots of things in life, but time isn't one of them. Fortunately, I realized this at a relatively young age, and veered off a career path that was leading me deeper into the urban jungle and farther away from the woods and waters of my native northern Minnesota. When Vikki and I moved to Lake Superior's North Shore in 1987, we were sure of one thing: We were where we wanted to be.

We were less sure that we could survive on the Shore. I'd worked on magazines and, in Grand Marais, as a newspaper editor, but what I really wanted to do was write about conservation and the outdoors. Making a living as an outdoor writer is a chancy proposition, especially when you live in the middle of nowhere. I took the chance and have never regretted the decision. The North Shore is still our home.

We live in Hovland, a small community 20 miles from the nearest gas station or grocery store. It's a place where moose occasionally walk through the back yard and you may hear a wolf howl when you let the dog out at night. The weather is cool in the summer and cold in the winter, but we don't mind. This is a warm community. The greatest reward of a writing life is having the opportunity to live in a place like this and getting to know its people, many of whom we met by becoming involved in the Hovland Volunteer Fire Department. You'll meet some of our Hovland neighbors in the pages of this book. You'll also be introduced to our dogs, our friends, and our family. Although Vikki and I live in a remote place, we are never lonely.

During the time we've lived here, the North Shore has changed, and not for the better. Residential and recreational development has spread like a cancer along the coast. The wild character that once defined this place is increasingly tamed— even the rutted logging roads now have street signs. But the wild still exists, if you are willing to seek it out. Along the trout streams, back in the moose meadows, and in the track- less forest beyond the official hiking trails is a wild world few people see. If you can read a compass or paddle a canoe, you can get there.

Let's go.

Shawn Perich

Hovland, Minnesota

January, 2004

Out in
the Cold

Faster, Slushbag!

"You're weird."

Six-year-old Ryan Lenski has emerged from his fishing tent and trudged 50 yards across the ice to make this pronouncement. We are fishing for lake trout. Ryan hasn't had a bite all morning. I'm the target of his boredom.

"You're weird," he says again.

This is my fault. A half-hour earlier, I'd told him the same thing when he peeked through the window of his tent and giggled as I walked by. Apparently, he likes the way the word rolls off his tongue.

"You're weird," he says once more.

"How about if I turn you upside down and stick you head-first into a snowbank?" I ask.

Ryan giggles. "You're weird."

Ryan and his father Pete, of Silver Bay, and I are enjoying an impossibly warm Saturday in February. We've returned to a Gunflint Trail lake where fishing was good the weekend before. It is so warm that Ryan can make snowballs. Then he winds up and throws them at my face from a distance of four feet. I turn my head to avoid them, but every snowball goes wide of the mark.

Finally, I don't turn for a throw–and catch a faceful of sloppy snow. This is by far the funniest thing Ryan has seen all morning.

"How about if we send you down one of these ice holes and you can look for fish?" I ask.

"You're weird...Slushbag," he replies.

"Ryan, maybe you should settle down for awhile," his father wisely advises.

We have begun this day with high expectations, trudging out on the fog-shrouded lake at first light. We have drilled a series of holes along the edge of a reef in depths ranging from less than 20 to over 40 feet. We are using jigs and lines baited with live suckers. Though I missed a hard bite almost immediately, the action is slow. Finally, Pete lands a laker about 16 inches long–typical fare here. Lunkers lurk in this lake, but the ones we catch generally weigh less than two pounds. You can't beat them in the pan.

The fish are finicky, as they were the week before. They toy with our baits and we feed them minnows when we unsuccess-fully set the hook. At lunchtime, we have only a couple of them on the ice. When I reach into the fish house for a sandwich, Ryan is munching on chocolate chip cookies.

You might think that slow fishing would be intolerable for a six-year-old, but Ryan has plenty of enthusiasm. His father makes sure his fishing experiences are comfortable and fun. Ryan has a rabbit fur hat and warm winter clothes. The week before, Pete shopped from Duluth to Grand Marais to find Ryan a pair of warm boots. Pardon the pun, but this attention to detail keeps his kid from getting cold feet about fishing.

After lunch, the action picks up. I continue to feed them min-nows, but the Lenskis are putting fish on the ice. When Pete hooks a trout he lets Ryan reel it in. Or if he misses a strike, he lets Ryan fish in the hole. Often, lakers return for a second swipe at the bait. The fish seem to be located in depths of 30 to 40 feet. We keep augering new holes and moving about. Often, we get a bite just after dropping a line down the hole. Our catch slowly grows.

Today is Pete's day. He's having steady action and catching (or at least hooking) the most fish. The week before, Ryan and I caught all the trout. This didn't surprise Ryan.

"I'm a better fisherman than my Dad," he'd told me matter-of-factly as I pulled him off the lake on a plastic toboggan. "One time I caught seven walleyes before he caught one."

Yup, this kid is a fisherman–and a heck of a boaster, too.

As the afternoon wears on, the lake trout seem to move into deeper water. In the area where I'm fishing, they stop biting. I cut more holes, but can't find a hungry trout. Fishing further out from the reef, Pete and Ryan are still getting bites.

We have seven trout on the ice–two short of our combined limit–when I start cutting holes in deeper water. I still can't find a hungry trout, so I keep moving deeper. Finally, I'm parallel with Pete in 40-some feet of water.

Pete has a trout pecking at his bait and calls for Ryan. I lower a sucker minnow to the bottom and jig it with short twitches. Once I raise it up six inches and let it settle back down. My line stays slack. Hmmm...

Slowly, I lift the line until it's tight and set the hook. Moments later, I pull a 16-inch laker through the hole. While I'm unhooking it, Pete and Ryan are doing battle with another. Soon that fish–number nine–is on the ice.

Pete looks at me. It is 3:05 p.m.

"Should we throw one back and keep fishing for a big one?" he asks.

"I hate to quit on such a beautiful day."

It's a tempting suggestion. We consider staying, but decide to call it a day. We pack up. Ryan climbs into the toboggan so I can tow him back to the truck.

"I don't know if I can pull you after all you ate for lunch," I tell him.

"I didn't eat lunch. I ate ninety cookies," he answers.

"You're gonna look like the Pillsbury Doughboy."

Ryan giggles. "You're weird. Go faster, Slushbag."

Oh, the abuse...

Stalked by a coyote?

Lake Superior can fool you. On my way to the Twin Cities, I saw no firm ice anywhere along the North Shore. It was the first week of March, so I told folks attending my steelheading seminars at sporting goods stores there'd be no ice fishing for Kamloops rainbows this winter. Driving home, I saw portable fish houses off Duluth. The blanket of ice extended all the way to Hovland.

This late ice isn't unusual. Most years, the main body of Lake Superior doesn't make ice until February or March. The bitterly cold winter of 1993-94 was an exception. The entire lake froze that year. During the six years we'd lived on Lake Superior's shore, this was the first time the ice in front of our house was safe for walking and skating. By late February, there was 20 inches of clear, blue ice.

One morning in early March my neighbor called to say that his water line was frozen. Along the shoreline there, most everyone draws household water directly from the lake, using a submersible pump anchored to the bottom and water pipe protected from the surf with heavy, steel well casing. Extending through the length of the pipe is an electric heating element that keeps it from freezing in the winter. My neighbor worried the ice was frozen right to his pump, but he remained opti-

7

mistic. A transplant from Indiana, he was confident spring was on its way. I tried to curb his optimism by predicting that we'd be iced in for another six weeks. That afternoon, a strong wind started blowing out of the southwest. Soon blue water appeared about a half mile offshore. The blanket of ice began to heave, buckle and break up into truck-sized chunks. Within five minutes, waves were crashing on the shoreline rocks...fooled again.

I was sorry to see the ice go. The frozen lake is a highway for coyotes and timber wolves. I watched coyotes, alone or in packs of up to four animals, pass by daily from our picture windows. After a while, I could recognize individual animals. One evening just after sunset, I watched three coyotes howl and dance on the ice as they serenaded the neighbor's dogs. Judging from their tracks–and because we rarely saw them–the timber wolves usually took to the ice at night. But they were never far away. On some evenings when I walked the dog on the ice, I simultaneously heard barking dogs, yapping coyotes and howling wolves along the shoreline ridge.

Why are these wild dogs so attracted to the ice? Perhaps they're hungry. When the snow is deep in the woods, all the deer along the North Shore are yarded up close to Lake Superior, so the ice provides hunting coyotes and wolves a convenient way to sneak up on the whitetails. Or maybe they're looking for love. Late winter is the mating season for wild canines, so the frozen lake is like a coyote singles bar.

Either theory could explain the coyote behavior I witnessed one Sunday afternoon. Two coyotes left an offshore pressure ridge where I'd seen them bed down that morning and headed for shore, about a half mile west of our home. On a whim, I leashed Casey, then a gangly, nearly grown yellow Lab pup, and walked out on the ice. We were immediately noticed. One coyote continued into shore, while the other stopped and sat down to watch us.

I started roughhousing with Casey, whose nickname is "Slammer," because he's a full-body-contact kind of dog. Soon he was leaping, growling, and having a good time. The sitting coyote gave us its undivided attention. Then I faked a stumble and dropped to the ice. Slammer charged with enthusiasm...and the coyote broke into a trot. Using piles of broken ice for cover, the coyote quickly moved forward, stopping occasionally to survey the situation and–I assume–make sure the dog was still winning.

About a quarter mile out, the coyote disappeared behind a pressure ridge of broken ice that extended all the way to our location. I continued to lay on the ice and fight with the puppy for about five minutes. The coyote didn't reappear. Finally, I decided to stand up and look around. The animal was sitting on the other side of the pressure ridge, just 50 yards away. I shouted and waved my arms, but it didn't go away. The coyote watched while I walked with the dog (who never saw it) up to the house. It hung around for another five minutes, then trotted across the ice.

Some might call the coyote's behavior menacing. Bold is a better definition. I doubt the coyote could smell us, but was probably attracted to our movements. Obviously, it wasn't threatened by our presence, although from 50 yards the animal certainly identified us as a man and a dog. Was it just curious? Only the coyote knows.

On the crust

We didn't need to see them. The snap-crackle of breaking branches and the crunch of heavy hooves on crusted snow was unmistakably the sound of a startled moose–or two. We were separated by a stone's throw of heavy brush.

Casey, the woods-wise yellow Lab, and Abby, the half-grown German shepherd, paused on the trail ahead of me and listened. The crackle and crunch stopped. In the heavy cover, a moose was likely swiveling its ears, trying to get a fix on us and no doubt wondering if we belonged to the neighborhood wolf pack. The crackle and crunch began again, going north. Leaving moose alone is a matter of respect–and common sense. The dogs know the drill. We went another way.

Out in the woods the roaming is easy. The snow, softened by warmth and rain during a March thaw, is now frozen hard as concrete, making the forest one big sidewalk. Recently emerged from semi-hibernation, I need exercise every day. So do the dogs. Most nights before supper, we hike the overgrown logging roads near home. Sometimes we climb the south-facing ridge above Lake Superior to look for deer antlers. A week ago, Vikki came with us to a quiet, stone beach where there are some "Pukaskwa pits" built by people who lived here very long ago.

Yesterday, we followed fox tracks in the snow. It's mating season for wild canines, and the fox's musky scent hung in the cold air. The dogs stopped to investigate every bush the fox had passed. The day before, we had come upon two-day-old tracks left behind by several timber wolves. The pack may have denned near our home last summer, because on several July evenings I heard the deep moan of a wolf howl and the barks and yips of puppies chiming in. In early winter, the pack was larger–nine walked past a friend's deer stand–but now it seems to contain five or six wolves.

On one trail, a wolf deposited a large, dark dropping. Spend much time in the woods and you become a student of such things. This one bristled with deer hair. So far this winter, we haven't found any places where the wolves had killed a deer, although the other day Abby found a weathered splinter of a whitetail femur and carried it like a bone cigar. In another month, after the snow melts, we'll hike along the rock outcroppings above the lake and look for the patches of hair and bone fragments that mark the winter's kills.

This winter was an easy one for deer, although there aren't many of them. Scattered in small groups, they've had no problem moving about or finding food. In midwinter, I passed through a stand of jackpines on a ledgerock ridge where the deer had pawed through the shallow snow, apparently to feed on lichens.

Of course, the dogs see–and smell–different things than I do. Casey detours through every blowdown and balsam thicket in search of sulking grouse. He knows we're not hunting, but he's still a bird dog. Abby, on the other hand, just likes to romp and run. If she can occasionally catch up with Casey and tug on his ear, so much the better.

The three of us can cover a lot of ground in an hour or so. We come out of the woods panting hard and ready for supper. It's a great way to work up an appetite.

Duane's trout

If ice fishing were figure skating, Duane and Virginia Johnson of Hovland would be the team to watch. They've been fishing together so long that they have a flawless routine. Call it poetry on ice...or something like that.

Recently, the two of them were ice-fishing for lake trout on a lake along the Canadian border. The action wasn't fast, but with persistent jigging, they'd put a couple of pan-sized lakers on the ice. At lunchtime, Duane moved to another hole in 30 feet of water. Twice he missed a light bite on his jig, but the third time was the charm. He set the hook into a fish that was more than pan-sized.

"It just started to run," said Duane.

His fishing reel was spooled with 150 feet of eight-pound monofilament, with 20-pound-test braided line for backing. Pretty soon, the braided line was headed down the hole.

"The fish would run 25 to 50 feet into my backing," Duane said.

It was obvious that he'd tied into a whopper. He glanced at his watch, which read 12:50, and estimated he'd already played the fish for about five minutes. Then he settled in for the fight. He was unable to get the fish within 100 feet before it made another run. Sometimes, he'd go 10 minutes without gaining any line at all.

Virginia watched the battle for a while. Then, bored, she went back to fishing. So much for poetry. She caught two more small lakers, while Duane continued his Hemingway-like struggle with the leviathan beneath the ice. Eventually, the line tightened and wouldn't budge. For about 10 minutes, Duane figured the fish had wrapped the line around a log. Then he discovered the knot between the line and backing was wedged in a crack in the ice at the bottom of his hole. He pushed the rod tip down and worked it free.

Surprisingly, the big fish was still on the line. The trout was starting to tire. Duane reeled it closer. A few bubbles came up the six-inch-diameter hole. Now things got tricky. The pooped-out trout was just beneath the ice, but Duane couldn't turn its great head into the small hole. Every time he tried, the fish turned sideways and all he could see was its gill plate–so close, yet far away beneath two-and-a-half feet of ice.

Now comes the poetry part. Virginia did some quick thinking. She tied a big Swedish Pimple to her line and managed to hook it inside the trout's mouth. Together, the couple turned the trout's head and pulled it into the hole.

"It was a tight fit," said Duane.

Indeed, it was tight enough that the Johnsons weren't sure they could tug the fish through the ice. So, again thinking quickly, Virginia reached down to her elbow in the icy water and stuck her hand inside the trout's open mouth.

"I told her not to do it, because she'd cut her hand, but she did anyway," said Duane.

With a quick pull, Virginia lifted the trout the rest of the way through the hole. And she did cut her hand in the process. Duane looked at his watch again. It was now 2:37. He'd played the lake trout for nearly two hours. Duane figures the trout may have won had not Virginia lent her hand.

14

"Without my wife's help, I wouldn't have caught it," he said.

The lake trout weighed 19 pounds and had nearly straightened Duane's small, light-wire hook. His jig was hooked at the hinge of the trout's jaws, which may explain a couple of things. First, a fish hooked that way can turn its head and get leverage against the angler. Battling a trout hooked in the corner of the jaw is like trying to pull against the flat side of a plank. This is probably why Duane had trouble getting the fish started into the hole.

Duane says the fish was "a good-looking trout," a definition any experienced lake trout angler will understand. The trout's flesh was as red as a salmon and delicious when it came out of the Johnsons' smoker. Although it was the biggest fish he'd ever caught through the ice and the longest he'd ever played a fish, Duane didn't consider mounting it. He says he caught plenty of trout that size and bigger 40 years ago on Lake Superior. As far as beating long odds to ice this trout, Duane was nonchalant.

"It was a long ordeal, but a fun one," he said of the battle. "I guess that's what a guy lives for."

Break up

Spring moves north

I've got spring fever.

This morning I drove 20 miles to Grand Marais, crossing a half dozen creeks that were washed awake from their icy winter sleep by April's first rain. The snow along their banks was dingy, dirty, and going fast. Good riddance. Some folks call this mud season. If you have kids or a dog, the next few weeks are an endless mop-up operation, because everyone is making tracks across the floor. Oh well, it beats shoveling snow.

I don't mind the mud. In fact, I'll spend the next few weeks slogging around in it. Spring days are longer and there is so much to do. Early mornings are spent along the creeks, soaking spawn sacks for steelhead. In the afternoon, I walk the dogs in the woods and look for deer and moose antlers. In between, I meet deadlines and toil in the yard. Work and fun always get done, because spring is so energizing. From now until the snow flies I spend less time sleeping, just to take advantage of all the extra daylight.

This doesn't mean that spring on the North Shore is all warm and wonderful. Stinging April rains are followed by mud-stiffening cold snaps that last for days or weeks. Sometimes it snows in May. Night ice forms on Lake Superior until June. But these chilly remissions cannot stop the season's progression. In the North, spring moves forward to the drumbeats of ruffed grouse perched like feathered kings on secluded, mossy logs. It grows with the sudden freshness of new, green grass. Everything happens so quickly that if you don't get outside, you can miss it.

That's why I start early and go late. After a long, white winter, I just can't get enough of the new sights, smells, and warm breezes. Perhaps tonight I'll go out at twilight and listen to the woodcock performing their twittering mating flight. And maybe, after dark, I'll take a flashlight and look for dew worms. Tomorrow, weather willing, I'll take them fishing. Oh yes, there's lots to do now, and precious little time to do it. Before you know it, black fly season will be here.

No snobs among spawn soakers

From the back yard, toiling with rake and pruning shears, I can hear the arrival of trout season. Nearby, the Flute Reed River is running fresh and vibrant as it breaks free from the shackles of winter ice. To a trout fisherman, this is music. Soon the big rainbow trout we call steelhead will run up from Lake Superior to spawn.

It is time to make spawn sacks, the small clusters of orange-colored eggs that I use for bait at this time of year. Thawing in the kitchen sink is a slender packet of frozen trout eggs, saved from a hen rainbow trout I caught last spring. Prior to freezing, the eggs were carefully washed in cold water and dusted with borax, a natural preservative. Smaller than a pencil eraser, preserved trout eggs have a rubbery exterior and a squishy interior. They are surprisingly durable. Tonight I'll tie them into tiny mesh sacks.

Making spawn sacks is a sticky ritual that you endure because no bait works better for fresh-run steelhead. Invariably, a few eggs break and adhere to your fingertips as a fishy goo. Then the fine mesh, thread, and eggs used to make more spawn sacks stick to your fingers. The best quality eggs are the least sticky, so it pays to take good care of spawn that is your raw material.

I can tie up enough spawn sacks for a day's fishing, say three dozen, in just a few minutes. First I cut three-inch squares of nylon mesh that you can buy in tackle shops. Then I put a few eggs, about a dozen, in the center of the square. Picking up the corners of the mesh to form a small sack, I secure it with a few wraps of thread and a couple of half-hitches. The result is a thumbnail-sized sack that looks like a raspberry. The sacks are stored in a plastic container that fits in your pocket.

Not all who fish for steelhead use the stuff. Some anglers do nose crinkles and upper lip curls at the mere mention of spawn sacks. "I only use artificials," such an angler will say, in a tone that may range from veiled condescension to unabashed snobbery. These anglers consider the use of natural bait a character flaw. So be it. On the icy heels of a retreating winter, when cold numbs both fish and fisherman, natural spawn works much better than any artificial. Anyone who is crazy enough to go fishing then would be crazy not to use it. That is, if you can get it. You must first catch a fish to acquire spawn for bait, a Catch-22 that stymies rookie anglers. Another irony is that you can fool a trout to its demise with the eggs of its kin. Dwell too long on that morbid twist of affairs and you may switch to artificials.

Catching steelhead is a skill honed with experience. Each steelhead you catch makes it easier to land the next one. I like to use a stiff fly rod and 6- or 8-pound-test monofilament line. Snelled to the line is a very sharp, size 6 egg hook. I carefully slide the hook beneath the knot in the spawn sack to avoid puncturing the eggs. Then I pinch just enough split shot on my line so the spawn will sink to the bottom, but drift naturally with the current. The trick is to keep the spawn within a few inches of the river bottom, where the silvery rainbows rest on their migration. Although they don't feed during their spawning run, steelhead strike at enticing baits. Recognizing the subtle take, which occurs as your spawn bounces along the bottom, is a nearly paranormal reflex that steelheaders call "the touch." All the best anglers have it.

I could cast artificial flies in the early spring to satisfy the fishing purists, but who cares what they think? I enjoy standing on shelf ice, drifting a spawn sack through the frigid pools of an awakening river. The action is slow, but on every drift, you hope a mighty, silver rainbow will crush your spawn sack and battle like a Lake Superior storm. When the storm is subdued, you marvel at the fish, as firm and chrome as an ingot in your hands, and then let it go. It is a touch of the wild, not a meal, that most steelheaders seek.

Tonight I'll tie up spring's first spawn sacks and store them in a plastic bottle in the refrigerator. Tomorrow morning, as the sun rises over Lake Superior, I'll put that bottle in my jacket, pick up a fly rod, and go fishing. In a couple of weeks, after spring conquers winter, the river waters will warm up a few degrees and I'll switch to artificials. But until then, a humble spawn sack will be stuck on my hook. In April, it takes a flawed character to catch fish.

Antler serendipity

Three tines stuck up like bony fingers without a palm. Lying in the duff, most of the ancient moose antler was rotted away. Still, it was spring's first find. I carried it to a chest-high, fat stump along the game trail that is my pathway through this place. I'd stashed antlers there before.

I usually spend a few hours wandering around in this hellish tangle of blowdowns, tag alder swamps, cut-overs, and balsam thickets just after the snow melts. The abundance of browse and dense, sheltering cover creates five-star accommodations for wintering moose. I look for the antlers the bulls leave behind. This time, in two hours of tough walking, I found just that one old antler, oddly enough, in a spot where I've often walked before.

Antler hunting is serendipitous. You can walk for hours, miles, even days through "moosey" country without finding one. Suddenly you happen upon a beauty, lying on the ground as if it were waiting for you to arrive. When you find a moose antler, you are likely the first person who has seen it. Great or small, even half-chewed by critters, a moose antler is a prize find most folks will take home.

You can discover antlers by chance while grouse hunting

or picking blueberries, but most are found by the growing cadre of people who go out in the spring and look for them. Why hunt for antlers? Some folks are in it for the money. A matched pair of trophy-sized moose antlers may fetch upwards of two hundred dollars. The price per pound for antlers of lesser quality varies, but even old, chewed-up antlers are worth a few bucks. However, many antler hunters hoard their finds. Count me among them. I save the best ones, even though I'm not sure what I'll ever do with the growing heap. Like any miser, I find it hard to give up something that was so difficult to acquire.

On my second antler hunt, Casey, my yellow Lab, nosed a small palm lying along a skid trail as we emerged from a moose pasture of buggy-whip aspen and balsam saplings. The inside of the palm was gray from lying in the sun, so I assumed it was dropped two winters before. Evidently, no one had walked or driven an ATV along this skid trail since then.

On my third hike, again with canine assistance, I found two antlers just a few feet apart, likely dropped by a bedded bull. This is a big score in antler hunting. The only problem was, some critter found them first. The tips of the paddles were chewed off, perhaps by a bear, and the faded palms were stained pink from algal growth. The real bummer was I had passed less than 50 yards from this spot during the two previous springs—and the antlers likely were lying there.

Lugging antlers out of the woods is a chore. They're heavy, unwieldy, and have lots of points that hook the brush or poke you in the wrong places. Once, on an exceptionally productive afternoon, I carried four antlers about a half mile, first through blow down and then across a dense stand of broomstick aspen saplings. It was not a walk I would care to repeat, but will—whenever I'm again lucky enough to find four antlers.

Successful antler hunting is part luck, part skill, and mostly persistence. You must read the woods well enough to recognize winter moose cover and develop a knack for spotting shed antlers. But most importantly, you have to bust a lot of brush. Antler hunters are "woodticks," folks who are as comfortable in the forest as you are in your living room. Seeking sheds is not a pastime for those who think trudging along a marked hiking trail or cruising backroads with an ATV is a "wilderness experience." You have to step off the path to find an antler.

And that's why I keep looking for them.

Spring music

We have a lonesome woodcock in our back yard. In the evening, a male timberdoodle launches his mating flight from a grassy opening behind the house. I hear his insect-like "peent" sounds when I bring in firewood at sunset. If I pause and watch the sky, I see him spiralling upward on his mating flight like a tiny, crazy duck, to the accompaniment of soft, flute-like sounds made by his wings. Then, just as he is about to disappear from sight in the gloaming, he'll tumble back to earth, alighting again in the opening.

In the spruces across the road, another recent arrival is seeking a mate. The clear, trilling song of a cock robin is spring's evening serenade. Like the woodcock, the robin has a specific agenda: find a mate, build a nest, raise a family and get the heck out of northern Minnesota before the snow returns. You could say that at the moment our back yard–and yours–is nothing but a big avian lonely hearts club.

I like listening to the songs of birds on the make. Some I can identify, but recognizing the singer matters little to my appreciation of the tunes. In the spring, individual bird songs blend into an ever-changing symphony better than anything you'll hear at the Guthrie or Orchestra Hall. Call it the original open air concert.

29

Listening to bird music is a privilege. Vikki has hearing loss and for her, spring is as quiet as winter. In fact, when she began wearing hearing aids a few years ago, she marvelled, not so much at being able to understand what people were saying, but that she could again hear the birds singing, though softly. More audible for her are the resonating thumps of a drumming grouse, an ascending staccato of wingbeats. Several years ago I showed her how to sneak up on a drummer by focusing on the sound's direction and softly stepping forward every time the bird drummed. You can get very close if you're patient and stop whenever the bird is silent. Vikki was able to approach within a few feet of the drumming log without disturbing the bird. Then Mr. Grouse decided to put on a show. He hopped off the log and strutted over to her with his tail feathers fanned and his ruff flared, looking like a miniature tom turkey. Vikki was flattered by his attention.

A courting ruffed grouse acts like a gentleman, but some species are less suave. Have you ever watched the amorous antics of ducks careening in flight over a marsh? Drake mallards pursuing a hen behave like bikers at a beer party–I'll spare you the details. Many species have beautiful courtship rituals. Bald eagles in love are elegant. I once watched a pair perform an aerial mating ballet high above Big Lake on Wisconsin's Bois Brule. They'd dive, twist and lock talons; two regal birds enthralled in an ancient sky dance. The spectacle was humbling to behold.

Sights like that inspire you to count your blessings. In the spring, just being outside and doing something you enjoy is a precious gift. As the world awakens, so do your senses. Bird music, the intoxicating scent of balsams and warmth of the sun on your face are sensations as fresh as a dandelion blossom. The other night, watching the woodcock twitter across the dusky sky, I pondered for a moment the wonder of the world around me. What had been important all day suddenly became insignificant. All that really mattered was embodied in a tiny, lonesome bird. I watched him disappear in the twilight and then carried my armload of firewood inside.

City boy goes native

Since the resort where we planned to stay is booked full, we may camp out on our annual Canadian trout fishing trip. This is not welcome news to at least one member of our party.

"Vince says he'll still go if we camp, but he won't enjoy himself nearly as much as if we stay in a cabin," read today's e-mail from another member of our crew.

Vince is not a camping kind of guy. He's a big city boy who likes to fish, preferably on nice days when they're really biting. Après trout, he prefers a hot shower, a comfortable chair, a cigar, and 70 decibels of Alanis Morrisette. When we introduced him to fishing in Canada, he stepped out of the tent on the first morning with a blow dryer and asked where to plug it in. His camping experience went downhill from there. This was due to circumstances largely beyond Vince's control. "Camping" on one of our excursions is better described as living a hunter-gatherer lifestyle with the benefit of a pickup truck.

Our philosophy is simple: In this life, you are allotted only so much time to go fishing; might as well make the most of it. We start fishing at first light and quit at nightfall. Supper is whatever you can heat up on a Coleman stove or sear over an open fire. Sometimes we set up a base camp with ancient umbrella tents. Often, though, we roam about and camp wherever darkness finds us. These are rugged bivouacs. If you live close to the earth, as we do on these trips, you become very attuned to the weather. When the sun shines, you fish in comfort and spring is wonderful. When a numbing north wind blows, your hands get cold and ice collects in your fishing rod guides. And when you wake up in a soaked sleeping bag to a pouring rain, you never dry out.

On Vince's first night under the stars, the temperature dropped far below freezing. Then we got him up before daylight with no place to blow-dry his hair. At least the weather warmed, although it started raining the second day. On the third morning out, Vince woke to a command. "Put your waders on Vince, we're flooding out," said his tent mate, who was already standing outside in his waders and rain gear. Fortunately, the other tent was warm and dry, so the rest of our crew enjoyed a laugh at Vince's bedraggled expense. It was better than the blow-dryer.

Picture a guy who's never gone a day without a shower three days into a fishing trip that's like a scene from "Quest for Fire." Now toss in a sodden sleeping bag, soggy clothing, and companions who have no time to offer sympathy because they are going fishing–rain or no rain. The expression "not a happy camper" aptly described Vince. On our fourth and final night we rented motel rooms–not from pity, but because our camp was washed out. Vince showered, ate a restaurant dinner, and seemed better for it.

Since then, we've gone easy on him. On his second Canadian trip, we rented a ramshackle house trailer at an old resort–just so Vince could blow-dry his hair. Oddly enough, he towel-dried his head like everybody else. Last year, he cheerfully went five days without a shower. The only problem was that he stayed at my house. I guess we've finally got Vince working pretty well in the field. Now all we have to do is housebreak him.

No secrets in the women's department

Sometimes you're in the wrong place at the wrong time. I'd stopped in the Grand Marais DNR office to get a moose hunt application (oddly enough, they don't have them) and was shooting the bull with the wildlife biologists. It was late on a Friday afternoon. The fisheries and forestry staff had already gone home. Two guys who looked like they'd stepped out of an upscale fly-fishing catalog walked in.

"Where can we find brookies and rainbows?" one asked.

Wildlife biologists, Dave and Bill pled ignorance.

"I hardly ever go fishing," Bill said.

The pair was not easily dissuaded. Determined to get some local information, they turned to me.

"Go west of Grand Marais," I advised.

"The Temperance? Poplar? Cascade?" asked one, naming three rivers they'd crossed on Highway 61.

"All of those systems are good," I replied.

"I notice you sent them west of Grand Marais," Dave said.

Coincidentally, I live 20 miles east of town.

33

The next day, the pair stopped at Joynes Department Store in Grand Marais, where Vikki works–and fields fishing questions from the women's department. She sent them to my favorite steelhead river east of Grand Marais. Thanks, dear.

Endless
Twilight

In the company of loons

The trout in the tiny lake were the best kind: big and diffi-cult to catch. They slashed the surface like spotted sharks, avoiding my flies with maddening disdain. Such fish catch the fisherman. I drifted on a still bay, casting and retrieving with predatory concentration. A few minutes before, a two-pounder had made off with my last fly of the only pattern that drew strikes from these perplexing fish. The fault was mine–striking too hard–and I watched silvery flashes beneath me as the freed trout tried to shake the fly from its jaw.

Now dejected, I was just pitching flies in a losing game. I studied the water, looking for some clue that would help me punch the trout's meal ticket. Suddenly, a stream of air bubbles tickled the still surface about 20 feet away. Trout don't burp, but I was about to lay a curious cast on the bubble stream when a loon surfaced there. Our eyes instantly met–a taboo in the wild–and with a startled yelp and a splash the great bird dove.

It surfaced again, further away. This time it sized me up, swimming with wary grace. The bird was sleek and shiny, its long bill like a metallic harpoon. Evidently deciding I posed no threat, it casually dove and disappeared. Both of us went back to our fishing.   Hopefully, the loon was luckier than I was. Fishless, I came ashore as the midsummer twilight deepened into darkness. Across the lake, where we'd met, the loon sang. Its voice echoed on the ridges, a haunting sound that sent an involuntary–and not unpleasant–chill down my spine. My feet found the darkened path that led to the truck. I enjoyed the walk for its wildness.

Wild puppies

All ears, all feet. That's the best way to describe the timber wolf pup we met the other day, trotting down a gravel road. As we approached in the truck, the little wolf–hardly the size of a red fox–disappeared in the brushy ditch.

"Get your camera," I told Vikki as we pulled up beside the place where we last saw the pup. "Maybe we can get a picture."

I stepped out and walked to the edge of the road, surprising the pup in the ditch. It scurried into a hazel thicket. When Vikki walked up, I went into the woods to see if the pup was still there.

"Oh, there it is!" she said.

The pup had popped back out about 50 yards down the road and was trotting away. I whistled, and the wee wolf paused and looked back. Then it bounded into the ditch and, as we drove nearer, disappeared in the woods. The pup seemed to be all alone, even though the little critter was too young to be on its own–easy pickins for a bear, a fox, an eagle, or a trigger-happy yahoo. We wondered if we should've tried to catch it, but decided that it was probably against the law to capture a wolf even if you were trying to save its life. We hoped the pup's mother would come looking for it. Unfortunately, friends of ours saw it in the same place the next day. The pup still seemed unwilling to leave the road.

At this time of year, you encounter wild puppies along the backroads. After dark on a recent evening, I spied a fox pup while driving home from fishing. I turned the truck so the headlights illuminated the brushpile where the pup took refuge, and then got out. Too young to be fearful, the pup let me approach within 20 feet. I crouched and started squeaking like a mouse. The pup cocked its head and looked curious. Out of the corner of my eye, I saw some motion. Across the road, another pup was watching me too.

The second one was suspicious of this monster mouse that had climbed out of the iron moose. It watched me intently for a few moments, and then ducked into the high grass. The pup in the brushpile, however, was enthralled with my squeaks. I edged closer, but it warily backed up. Then it vanished into the brushpile, only to peek out and see if I was still there.

"You shouldn't be so curious," I told the pup. "The next person you see might not be so friendly."

Hopefully, the pup heeded my advice. Yes, that tiny fox might grow up to eat a grouse or two, but I was smiling when I drove away.

Hoodoo hides in canoe

"You're a hoodoo," says Gord Ellis.

It is the sort of cocky remark you hear when sharing the canoe with a fisherman who has caught three brook trout and you've landed none. The moniker is not original. Gord learned it earlier in the day from my father, who joined us on this fly-in excursion to Paul Morgan's Blue Fox Camp in northern Ontario. Dad, in turn, picked it up from a friend of mine. "Hoodoo" is not a term of endearment, but the people who fish with me take no prisoners.

Ellis, an Ontario outdoor writer and passionate brook trout angler, is tossing small spoons, while I force fly casts into a stiff breeze. We are fishing one of the many small lakes scattered in the hills around Blue Fox. All contain brookies, including some big ones. Before we arrived, an angler landed a 7 3/4-pound speck from this lake. We are looking for similar fish.

So far, the fish Ellis has landed are around 15 inches long, respectable brookies, but not lunkers. Still, after listening to his jibes, any trout on the end of my line would be welcome. But fish avoid me. On an evening troll for lake trout in Blue Lake, where the camp is located, Ellis lands a three-pounder. Dad and I reach the dock at dark, skunked.

"You're a hoodoo," says Ellis.

All three of us have tough fishing the next day, when the wind blows with such force it is difficult to paddle a canoe, much less fish from it. Ellis, of course, blames the weather on me. That evening, as the wind subsides, I finally connect with some lakers. I feel better for it.

Nevertheless, Ellis remains convinced that I'm dogged by a hoodoo and continues with his now razor-honed verbal jabs. I'm not only a hoodoo. Now I've become an "ugly American." After all, I still haven't caught a brook trout. As my fishless bell tolls, his Canadian cockiness climbs to a new level. In a conversation about backcountry canoeing, he makes a bold pronouncement.

"In 37 years," he says, "I have never fallen out of a canoe."

The hoodoo was listening.

The next morning we decide to try a lake where I've caught three-pound brook trout in the past. The wind has let up and fishing conditions seem promising. We set off in two canoes. Ellis and I share one. My father and Jay, our guide, share the other. We paddle the perimeter and cast without getting a strike. Ellis and I go to shore where a creek enters the lake. Almost immediately, he catches a 16-incher. The hoodoo stuff starts up again.

When Jay and Dad arrive, we decide to go exploring. An overgrown trail leads to a lake where Jay says a provincial fisheries crew reportedly netted five-pound specks the previous fall. No one from Blue Fox–or likely anyone else–has fished there. We decide to carry in one canoe and give it a try.

The lake is a clear-water gem, ringed by towering white pines. I push off in the canoe with Jay, while Dad and Gord cast from the ledgerock shore. Jay paddles slowly, while I cast into the bank with a small spinner. Nothing happens.

Rummaging through my tackle, I find a tiny Half Wave spoon that has been in my box since I bought it in Atikokan, Ontario at age 10. In a moment of whimsy, I tie it on. Casting to a tangle of downed trees along the shore, my retrieve stops with a thump.

"This is a big one," I tell Jay.

The fish stays deep. When it finally flashes beneath the canoe, we see it is a slab-sided brookie. We have no net. Eventually, I pull the tired trout beside the canoe, reach over, and land the five-pounder by hand. While taking a few photographs, my thumb nicks its gills and the trout starts to bleed. I have caught and released larger brook trout. But this mortally injured fish will go to the taxidermist.

Without making another cast, we paddle back to Dad and Gord so they can try for a big one from the canoe. We watch them work their way around the lake, eventually pausing at the downed trees where I caught the trout. In due time, they return, fishless. They saw several huge brookies roll on the surface, but couldn't draw a strike.

"I saw one that was bigger than the trout you caught," Dad says.

Jay and I have walked around the lake opposite the bay where we put in. Gord agrees to paddle across, drop off Dad, and then come back for us. The canoe disappears into the bay. We wait and wait for him to return. Finally, the canoe rounds the point. A wet and bedraggled Canadian paddles up to the rock where we wait. After 37 years, it appears that Gord has finally fallen out of the canoe. He admits to as much, but details of the momentous event are sketchy.

"I think your father had something to do with it," he says. "He probably won't mention it."

Wrong.

"You see that muddy water," Dad says as we come near. "Some big s.o.b was wallowing around out there."

Gord, who must attend a wedding, flies out that afternoon. He leaves in good humor, although he doesn't want to discuss hoodoos. With a humble, off-handed remark, I note that my one brook trout weighs more than all of his combined. After he leaves in a float plane, Dad tells the whole story.

"Gord was having trouble getting away from shore, so I gave him a little push," he says with a grin. "He was off balance, but he fought it. Too bad you weren't there with a camera. You could've snapped two or three pictures before he fell in."

Like a pair of ugly Americans, we share a laugh at Gord's expense.

And somewhere in the Canadian bush, a hoodoo was laughing, too.

Aroma therapy

Summer officially arrived at our house about 4:30 a.m., when we awoke to a chorus of droning mosquitoes in the bedroom. The home invasion occurred when the fire burned low and dozens of mosquitoes followed the source of heat down the fireplace flue. They were hungry and ferocious.

My counterattack was worthy of a war criminal. I sprayed Black Flag throughout the house and watched the poison send my winged enemies into tailspins. Victorious, I went back to bed, but my rest was punctuated by Vikki's occasional claps as she administered a coup de grace to the few survivors of my chemical assault. She takes no prisoners. A few years ago, we fought a pitched battle at dawn with a seemingly endless horde of the bloodthirsty beasts. Vikki hasn't forgotten that grim morning.

Some folks say the true test of living in the north isn't surviving the winter; it's whether you can put up with the bugs. Anyone who's carried a canoe across a portage while enveloped by swarming black flies knows what they mean. Winter makes you gradually go bonkers from cabin fever. Black flies and mosquitoes can reduce you to a babbling idiot within minutes.

Black flies pack a lot of trouble into a tiny package. A typical black fly bite swells up to a dime-sized welt and doesn't go away for days. The little fiends are especially fond of tender places like behind the ear and around your ankles. If they really chew you up, you may feel out of sorts for a day or two. I once saw a Labrador retriever swell up around the eyes and muzzle and become physically ill after a five-minute encounter with black flies at a boat landing. Mom brought the swelling down by sponging the dog with baking soda and water where he'd been bitten.

Some folks swat and curse at biting insects. You may as well shout, "Dinner time!" All that commotion just attracts more bugs. A better approach is to pay no attention to them. They won't go away, but with practice you can tolerate surprisingly buggy conditions. When the insects get pesky, put on some bug dope with a high concentration of DEET, the active ingredient, to hold bugs at bay. DEET is strong stuff and some folks are uncomfortable using it on their skin, but it beats most home remedies. Consider the backwoodser who told me he avoids baths and stands near smoky fires during the bug season. After a few days, not even the black flies want him.

Cigars are equally aromatic and somewhat more socially acceptable. In fact, puffing on a cigar while trout fishing may be the only time when smoking is actually good for you. The northwoods' finest mosquito and black fly habitat is found along brook trout streams. And the fishing is best when the bugs are the worst. My cigar-smoking friends say the immediate relief from insects provided by a cigar smudge outweighs any long-term health risks. I wonder what the Surgeon General would say about that?

Of moose and mayflies

"Northwoods walleye anglers battling extended mayfly hatch," boomed a recent sports-page headline. Bummer, thought I, and went fishing.

The mayfly in question is a big, yellow-green bug that hatches from silt-bottomed lakes and streams at sunset, often in such abundance that walleyes and other fish gorge on them—to the exclusion of such tantalizing treats as leeches and nightcrawlers hung from hooks. Walleye anglers wail and gnash their teeth because the mayflies foil their fishing. But for fly-fishers like me, the mayfly hatch is the height of the season.

My destination this evening was a lonely place where quick currents meet still water. Hungry brook trout gather there at sunset. I arrived just before their dinner hour, as the sun sank into the spruces. Slathered with mosquito repellent, I quietly waded to a position where my backcast wouldn't tangle in bankside brush. Then I tied on a fly, a homemade, high-floating concoction of deer hair, moose mane, and chicken feathers that looks enough like a mayfly to fool a trout.

Heronlike, I waited.

The first rise was beside a table-sized cluster of lily pads. The cast was easy, maybe forty feet. My fly was resting on the water before ripples from the rise subsided. Moments later, it disappeared in a swirl. My fly rod bowed against stubborn resistance.

The brookie didn't want to come in. It dove for the shelter of the pads and wrapped the leader around sturdy stems. I could feel it thumping on the end of the line, but couldn't dislodge it. Wading deeper, I reached the pads before the lapping water cleared the top of my chest waders. Using my foot, I broke the stems that held the leader. The brookie resumed battle. Patiently, I drew it to hand, then quickly released the pot-bellied 13-incher.

The hatch started. Solitary mayflies appeared on the water, drifting like tiny sailboats in the current. The larvae live in soft bottom soils and then, when midsummer days are longest, swim upward to emerge on the surface–Cinderella-like–as delicate mayflies. They pause there for long moments, splendorous bugs, then flutter away. Within a day, they will mate and die.

Another trout rose and a mayfly sailboat vanished in the swirl. I cast my fly so it would ride the lazy current past the waiting trout. The drifting fly went unnoticed, so I cast again. This time the trout rose to the fly. I struck and missed it.

The flurry of action was short-lived. Hatching mayflies and subsequent rises grew sporadic. Minutes remained before darkness drew a curtain on the fishing. In such a situation, fishing smart pays dividends. You watch for rises, then stalk and cast to what you assume is an active fish. Down where the current ebbed into the lily pads, a trout rose several times. I waded over there, but deep water kept me out of casting range. Instead, a short cast to a chub-like rise fooled a 12-inch brookie.

A fish rose where the quick water spilled in, so I waded up to the head of the pond. A 14-incher took the fly on the second cast. Another swirled in the riffle as I released the trout. As I prepared to cast to the riser, I heard rustling in the brush and heavy footsteps. The head of a cow moose emerged from the alders behind me.

"What do you want?" I asked.

She gave me the silent treatment. The cow appeared to be a dark-faced yearling, rather comely as moose go. She just stood there, so close that I could have scratched her nose with the tip of my fly rod. She probably wanted to stand in the pond and eat water lilies, but I was there first. We shared a moment of reckoning. No two close encounters with moose are the same. Moose needn't run away from you, are unpredictably moody, and not very bright. This one just seemed curious, so I went back to my fishing.

The other brookie rose and was hooked within a couple of casts. A scrapper, it ran from the shallow riffle to deeper water. We played tug-of-war for a minute or two, then I gradually gained line. The moose looked on. Maybe she made me self-conscious, because I lost the brookie at my feet.

Eventually, the cow stepped back into the alders, fortunately across the pond from the path leading to my truck. I kept casting until dark, winding up the evening with five brookies to hand, one to my feet, and several missed strikes. The moose was within earshot until I left.

Pity the walleye anglers.

Rebel

Rebel was a southern gentleman.

Vikki and I acquired the yellow Lab in Georgia, not long before we moved home to Minnesota and Lake Superior's North Shore. He was raised in the northwoods, but we attributed Rebel's special qualities to his southern heritage.

Reb attracted people. When out for a walk, strangers always came to pet and talk to him. In Georgia, a neighbor remarked, "He shore is a purty dawg!" On the North Shore, Vikki once came out of the grocery store to find that a couple had taken him out of her unlocked truck. They said they couldn't help themselves.

Rebel gained notoriety as an art critic when I described in the Grand Marais newspaper how he lifted his leg on a driftwood sculpture we discovered on the beach. Outraged artists deluged the paper with fiery letters. Most everyone else thought the dog had good taste.

Reb was my outdoor companion. We ice-fished for lake trout, prowled steelhead streams, and paddled the canoe country. He sat on the canoe's bow seat as I fly-fished for brookies, intently watching the dry fly and waiting for a rise. When a fish was on the line, his exuberance rocked the boat. Paddle discipline kept us afloat.

In the fall, we hunted hard. Reb's duck blind manners weren't perfect, but neither was his master's training technique. Although he retrieved everything from woodcock to Canada geese, Rebel's forte was flushing ruffed grouse and pheasants. I can still see him pogo-sticking through heavy prairie grass, in hot pursuit of a cagy Iowa rooster.

He never started a fight with another dog, but Reb sure finished some. He didn't fare as well in encounters with skunks and porcupines, and I pulled him away from Mexican standoffs with raccoons, mink, and once an enraged river otter. He enjoyed running black bears, because they were fast and left a good scent trail. One August afternoon he took off after one as we walked the Superior Hiking Trail. I was about to give up waiting for him to return when he appeared, tongue lolling and lathered. He walked right past me and started for the truck—tuckered out and ready to go home.

Although we kept an eye on him, Rebel occasionally wandered off. He was known to the county sheriff's department and sometimes they'd phone to report his whereabouts. One hot August day, he disappeared while I was washing my truck. Looking for him, I caught a musky whiff of bear scent and knew where he'd gone.

Not long afterward, the sheriff's department called to say someone reported a trucker had struck a beautiful white dog walking along the highway shoulder. I found Rebel laying dead in the ditch. That night, Vikki and I tearfully buried him in an aspen thicket where we often hunted grouse.

We have other dogs now, but Rebel is still with us. Steelhead fishing last spring, I heard the familiar jingle of dog tags behind me. There was no need to turn around.

"Hi, Reb," I said, and kept fishing.

Miller Creek

Miller Creek doesn't look like much where it runs through the concrete culvert beneath Duluth's Anderson Road. Spring, when the stream runs strong and boisterous, is about the only season when you might notice it. In summer, a modest brook flows–shaded and cool–beneath a tangled alder canopy, hidden from passing traffic.

The summer morning air was still chilly enough for a light jacket when we pedalled our bikes the mile or so to Miller's (as we called it) with our fishing rods taped to the crossbars. By the time we'd hidden our bikes in the dew-wet grass along Anderson Road we were soaked from the knees down. It didn't matter, because we'd soon be splashing and squishing along the creek. We fished so often during the summer that our sneakers never really dried out anyway. Our quarry was brook trout; tiny, speckled jewels that inhabit the creeks coursing through Duluth. Although we pursued them with the sort of relentless zeal possessed only by 12-year-old boys, there seemed an endless supply. At our house, fresh trout were frequently on the menu.

Miller Creek was a favorite among our fishing repertoire of neighborhood brooks and ponds. Although it flowed through suburban back yards, the creek belonged to kids. The muddy paths along the banks were worn deep by generations of trout fishing delinquents. My grandfather had swum and fished in this creek, further downstream, shortly after the turn of the century. He used to tell me how he and his friends had carried buckets of Miller Creek brookies to the Twin Ponds along Duluth's Skyline Drive. Grandpa said that several years later a neighborhood fisherman discovered the Twin Ponds trout, which by then were trophy-sized. The fisherman kept his discovery to himself, covertly fishing in predawn darkness. Eventually, though, the word got out. It always does.

We never got trophies, but we always caught trout. Downstream from Anderson Road were several pools where hungry, but cautious, brookies lurked. In a couple of places you could sneak up to large rocks, peek over them and see the trout swimming below. Some kids tried to catch these trout in their hands, but we always used a hook and line; it was more effective. The best place to fish was where the creek tumbled over a five-foot waterfall, creating a foaming, well-oxygenated pool. Quite often we'd see trout leaping like tiny salmon as they attempted to scale the falls. The leapers wouldn't bite.

In August, the creek's water no longer felt cool to the touch. Fishing was difficult, because the sluggish trout were struggling to survive in the warm water. The concrete culvert became a fishing hotspot, because the dark, cool cavern beneath Anderson Road drew the warmth-stressed brookies like a magnet. We spent hours wading through the culvert, using short, ultralight fishing rods so we could cast.

Kids who get wet and muddy intuitively understand how nature works. Despite their apparent abundance, we knew that Miller Creek's brook trout had a tough go of it. And we knew why. Brook trout don't ask for much other than springs and shady banks to provide a constant flow of cool water, but some folks didn't see the bogs and brambles along Miller Creek the way we did. We saw a wondrous, wild world populated with trout and frogs and snowshoe hares. They saw parking lots.

As I was growing up, progress came to roost along the Miller Creek watershed. A new airport was built on the headwater springs, and a nearby forest was clear-cut for an industrial park. Further downstream, tributary creeks were ditched and the meandering creek was channelized to accommodate roads and development. Retail blight spread like cancer along the stream. Upstream from Anderson Road, the places where 20 years ago you could hear grouse drum, are now shopping malls. The cool contributions Miller Creek received from alder swamps were replaced by polluted gutter wash from parking lots. Recently, plans were announced to build yet another retail store in a place that contains the creek's remaining cool springs. Brook trout still swim in Miller Creek, but fish biologists say this new development could be their coup de grace. The project must meet zoning requirements, but the regulations aren't sufficient to protect the trout.

It's hard for a trout fisherman to watch a stream die, especially one that was such an important—make that formative—part of your life. Below Anderson Road, the creek will still tumble through backyard brambles, but without brook trout it will be just a lifeless, feral ditch. Future generations of kids in my old neighborhood will be denied the simple adventure of going fishing. I suspect they'll grow up to be very different from me.

Piscatorially incorrect

The lawn was mowed, the garden planted, and we were hungry for fresh fish.

I wanted to dunk worms in a creek for brook trout. Perhaps this wasn't the "piscatorially correct" approach for a fly-fisherman like me, but I just wanted to have fun. Besides, I've never met a trout fisherman worth knowing who hasn't dirtied his fingers with a worm or two. So I grabbed some nightcrawlers and went fishing.

The sun was sinking into the trees when I parked the truck beside the bridge and dug out fishing gear. Cloaked in shadows, the creek was about two fly rods wide and running full from recent rains. There were no boot tracks in the path through the alders along the bank. Perhaps that's why the mosquitoes were so hungry. I caught the first brookie, a six-incher, on the second drift. A chunky 11-incher—a trophy in a stream like this—came a few drifts later, within a stone's throw of the well-traveled forest road. I started fishing downstream, getting bites on nearly every drift.

The brookies were big enough to grab a chunk of nightcrawler, but small enough that they were difficult to catch with a number six hook. I'd feel a tap and then watch the line move as the brookie darted about with the bait. After waiting a few seconds I'd set the hook, usually missing the fish. Even so, I caught a couple of brookies in every pool, keeping the ones that fatally swallowed the hook. Before fishing a quarter mile of the creek, I had my limit of ten. The 11-incher was the biggest.

There was still some light left in the day and time for more fishing, so I headed for a nearby walleye lake. This time, I left the worms in the truck and grabbed a canvas satchel stuffed with fly boxes. Now, fly-fishing for walleyes may not be "piscatorially correct" either, but on soft June evenings, it works.

A path through a stand of fat-trunked aspens led to the lake. It was dusky among the trees and the air was rich with the sweet scent of balsam fir. Three ring-necked ducks flushed when I reached the water and circled overhead in the twilight. I started casting with a black Wooly Bugger, the fly-fisher's version of a leech, where an inlet entered the lake.

The Wooly Bugger swam unscathed. But oddly enough, fish were rising off a nearby point. Peering into the dusk, I saw a big, yellow Hexagenia mayfly on the water. Could the risers be walleyes? I waded to shore and rummaged through my fly boxes. Unfortunately, my big dry flies tied to imitate Hexagenia were at home. The only floaters I found were a box of bluegill poppers. I pulled out a yellow one and tied it on.

Wading into the water, I saw a fish rise in the inlet channel. I made one cast, then another. The popper disappeared in a swirl. Whatever took the popper was strong enough to bow my five-weight fly rod. I played the fish carefully, curious to see what was on the end of the line. Eventually, I slipped my hand around a 14-inch walleye. Two casts later, I caught its twin.

Three more walleyes about the same size came in short order. Number six was smaller, so I threw it back. A few casts later, number seven was on the line. It ran and stayed deep, making my fly line knife through the water. We battled, then I pulled the 17-incher to hand. I caught and released one more walleye before darkness drew a curtain on the fishing. My feet hardly touched the trail on the walk out. What an evening! We had our choice of fresh walleyes or brook trout for dinner.

Call me piscatorially incorrect.

Call me a fish hog.

Just don't call me and ask where I was fishing.

An everyday hero

"It's a good thing the moose keep this trail open," said Stan Pelto.

With a flashlight, Pelto was leading Orvis Lunke and me down a seldom-hiked spur of the Border Route Trail, a hiking path that runs along the Canadian border in Minnesota's canoe country. The sun had set two hours ago. Dense brush, soaked by afternoon showers, obliterated the path and concealed endless deadfalls. Despite the darkness and obstacles, Pelto set a pace that most folks would consider fast on a city sidewalk. But then, Pelto, a logger, and Lunke, a forester, probably spend more time in the woods each year than most people do in a lifetime.

We had good reason to hurry. Somewhere ahead in the dark, lonely valley of Portage Brook, a 65-year-old woman was about to spend a cold and miserable night. On a day hike, she and a female friend had lost the Border Route Trail in a formidable tangle of blowdowns. Searching for the trail, she became exhausted and cramped, eventually encouraging her younger friend to continue without her. The friend had showed up at Pelto's home on the Arrowhead Trail just before dark. At 9:20 p.m., five of us from the Hovland Volunteer Fire Department and First Responders started the search. Volunteers from the

61

Cook County Search and Rescue Unit squad were on the way.

The country was new to me, so I just tried to keep up. Occasionally, Pelto would stop for a moment and use his flashlight to read the map or take a compass bearing. Then away he'd go. At Portage Brook we lost the trail and crossed the creek on a beaver dam. It didn't matter, because we were already soaking wet. We walked downstream until we found the hiking trail bridge and then followed the trail until it disappeared beneath a six-foot wall of balsam blowdowns. Lunke, who knew the area from his forestry work, led the way cross-country. We waded through waist-high raspberry thickets and tripped over slash in the clear-cuts. In the woods, we climbed over windfalls. Sometimes, we fell down. We called the woman's name, but heard no answer.

Eventually, we met up with the Rescue Squad. They'd come from another direction and driven two ATVs down a grassy logging road, winching across a bottomless mudhole along the way. Together, we searched the area where the Border Route Trail again became discernible, but we didn't find our hiker. Then the radio dispatcher in Grand Marais gave us another clue: The other woman said she'd left her friend on the banks of Portage Brook.

Lunke said the creek was "about a half mile away," and then led us through swamps and tangles for what seemed a bit further than a half-mile. But in the dark, who knows? At Portage Brook we spread out and searched west of the hiking trail bridge. We still didn't find her. After 2 a.m., the Rescue Squad decided to call off the search until morning, when a Minnesota State Patrol helicopter equipped with a heat-seeking device could provide assistance. It was after 4 a.m. before I got to bed.

In the northwoods, hypothermia is a serious risk even in August. Knowing the woman was unprepared to spend a cold, wet night outside worried Stan Pelto. At daylight, he started off alone. By the time I started up the Arrowhead Trail, both he and Lunke had already hiked to Portage Brook. Overhead, local bush pilot Russ Smith was searching with his floatplane.

About 8 a.m., Pelto came over the radio saying he'd heard a voice.

Then Russ Smith asked for a description of the woman's clothing. From the airplane, he guided Pelto to the hiker's location. Stan reached her at 9:20 a.m.; 12 hours after the search began. To everyone's relief, she was in excellent condition. She walked with Stan to a logging road, where they were met by the Rescue Squad's ATVs. Later, when I gave Stan a ride to his pickup, he said we'd passed within a quarter mile of the hiker during the night. I asked him why he'd started off by himself at dawn.

"I'm always up at that time," he said. "I wanted to get back in there while everything was still quiet."

Even though he'd missed a night's sleep, I doubt if Pelto took a nap when he got home. He probably hustled off to work. Everyday heroes are like that.

Smoke on Nipigon

The smoke drifted over Lake Nipigon on a shifting wind.

At first it was like a hazy overcast that you might think threatened rain. But the sunlight had a rosy ambience, a familiar glow that means somewhere the forest is burning. You could smell woodsmoke in the thickening haze.

We were miles offshore, trolling sunken humps near Big Flatland Island in Captain Bob Simpson's 25-foot sportfisher, the Miss Piggy. Beneath us lurked the giant lake trout for which Lake Nipigon is justly famed. In the first hour-and-a-half, we boated two fish with weights in the mid-teens. Simpson said yesterday's sports caught a pair of 30-pounders. We sought more of the same, as did others. Five boats worked the humps—a crowd on this northern lake.

Comparable in size to Lake of the Woods, Nipigon is deeper, colder, and wilder. Located north of Lake Superior, to which flows the mighty Nipigon River, the lake has very few launch sites along its wilderness shores. Simpson is among a handful of charter captains who specialize in catching its trophy-sized lakers. Last year, he came in with a fish topping 50 pounds.

We had a fine day for fishing, cooled by a breeze that stirred the lake to a light chop. The smoke, we surmised, came from a distant fire that presented no immediate threat. The other boats moved on, leaving us trolling the hump with just another boat, piloted by a lone angler called Turbo Al and his dog, Wrinkles.

"Hey, why don't you get Wrinkles a fishing rod?" shouted Bob as we passed the trolling Turbo. Over a crackling marine radio, Turbo told us he'd caught and released a 36-pounder.

We trolled on. Some say trolling with downriggers is boring, but big-water fishing is better described as an acquired taste, a form of fishing as quirky and challenging as any other. The downrigger is an electric winch that raises and lowers an eight-pound weight on a steel cable. A fishing line is clipped to the apparatus, allowing you to troll with standard tackle at great depths where lake trout dwell. While you troll, the rod rests in a holder. When a fish bites, the line pulls free from the clip. You pick up the rod and fight the trout unencumbered by the weight.

Between strikes, you can sit back and enjoy the boat ride. All anglers aboard take turns picking up the rod to fight fish. Our youngest angler, 11-year-old Ryan Lenski of Silver Bay, was up first. His father Pete, held on to his belt loop while he battled a big trout. Ryan was anything but bored.

We continued through a rotation. By the time the fourth member of our group, Charlie Uhrhammer of St. Paul, landed and released a 22-pounder, the smoke obscured surrounding islands. We were alone on a cold-water wilderness. Knowing our captain had 10 years of daily experience on Nipigon and that he used satellites to track our course on a GPS screen, we kept fishing.

Ryan was up again. There was a hard strike on the port rod, which pulled a huge, hammered Provisor spoon Simpson had special-ordered from Finland. As required by regulation, the lure's treble hook was barbless. You must be extra careful when you fight a big fish so the hook doesn't fall out. Ryan was onto a big one.

"Keep the rod tip pointing up," Simpson advised. "Don't allow any slack in the line."

Battling a monster lake trout is a team effort. Simpson's first mate, also named Bob, took the wheel. The boat must be maneuvered to keep the fish clear of the trolling gear and to avoid drifting over the line. Waiting with the landing net, Captain Simpson shouted instructions at Bob.

"Carve left! Hard left! Carve! Carve!" he cried. "Not so fast, you bloody bastard! Easy! Easy!"

Ahab, by comparison, was a schoolmarm. Ryan did a fine job on the fishing rod. Dad stood beside him as a quiet coach. The trout on the other end of the line was stubborn, staying deep and pulling strong. The butt of the rod was braced against Ryan's stomach to give him leverage over the fish. Minutes passed as he played the grudging trout, losing line when it made powerful dives, and slowly cranking it back.

Finally, the trout flashed deep in the clear water. The battle gained a visual dimension as Ryan fought the fish to boatside. In a flurry of shouts, quick steps, and tense moments, the laker was netted and brought aboard.

"It's a big one," someone said.

"Over thirty," said another.

No one disagreed.

A battle-weary kid showed his cramped hand, still cupped as though clenching the rod, for all to admire. The trout measured 42.5 inches long and 24.5 inches in girth. A handheld digital scale bounced by a pound or two just over 30 pounds. Working a weight formula based on length and girth, Simpson came up with 31 pounds.

Sometimes you know when a day of fishing reaches its apex. We kept trolling, even brought another trout to the boat, but we were just going through the motions. The breeze rose and blew the smoke off Lake Nipigon. The sun was shining on the long run in.

Dog
Days

Back-yard admiral

Sometimes, it's best to act first and explain later. In fact, that may be the only way to buy two boats in one week. At least it worked for me.

Vikki knew about the big boat. I'd been saving my money, looking at every boat we passed on the road, and regaling her with an endless monologue about the boat of my dreams for several years. She's patient and knows when to nod her head in agreement with my boating babble. Her biggest concern was that it had comfortable seats. It does. All it lacks, she tells me, is a windshield.

The second boat wasn't a surprise. She knew that I coveted my neighbor's square-stern Grumman canoe and four-horse kicker. She also knew that I'd asked if he planned to sell it. What she didn't know was that he'd decide to sell it the same week my other boat arrived—or that I'd saved a special fund with that contingency in mind. So I told my neighbor yes and then broke the news to Vikki.

"But you already have a boat," she said.

"Yes," I answered. "But I've wanted one of these square sterns for years. I can take it places where the big boat won't go."

"But you already have a canoe," said Vikki.

"Yes, but this canoe has a motor."

"But you already have an electric motor for your canoe," she said.

Obviously, she just didn't get it. Not only was there room for the square stern in my fleet, I flat-out needed it. The canoe with the putt-putt opened new horizons for fishing, duck hunting, and beaver trapping. I would be a motorized voyageur. Heck, one trapping expedition would probably pay for the thing.

If Vikki shared my enthusiasm she didn't show it. She has, however, been surprisingly obliging, even insistent, about properly rigging the big boat. All of our required safety gear is stowed on board. She bought me an anchor and a horn for my birthday. Play my cards right, and perhaps Santa will deliver a marine radio this Christmas. I have a pretty good first mate. Of course, she has been around this captain long enough to know this new boat was inevitable. She also knows that it will often be wet in the big waters of Lake Superior and the Nipigon system. She intends to do her best to ensure that the captain stays dry.

As for the captain, he's faced with a most pleasant task—making sure that two boats get some time on the water. He is pleased to report that the big boat arrived just at the time the trout started to bite on Lake Superior. He plans to investigate some nearby walleye waters with the putt-putt very soon.

Actually, "captain" is something of a misnomer. With the fleet at rest in the yard, "admiral" is more appropriate. However, I answer to both. And now, with the watercraft to effectively fish everywhere from the canoe country to Lake Superior, it is time for this admiral to again scan the far horizon.

What my fleet really needs now is a flagship.

Flogging the muskrat

Until recently, muskies and I were never formally introduced.

The toothy trophies are uncommon in waters where I fish. I'm mostly a trout and walleye guy (a "trout geek," according to a muskie-manic friend) who somehow avoided being bitten by the muskie bug—until it nipped me last week on Lake of the Woods. After two days of flogging the muskrat, I'm ready for more.

The "muskrat" was my name for the giant, black bucktail lure that Ray Ostrom of Bloomington gave me to cast for muskies. Built on a heavy wire, the bucktail had a huge spinner blade trailed by two monstrous treble hooks covered with mops of black hair. In the water, it looked like a muskrat swimming in the wake of a Toyota fender. Flogging the muskrat was the incessant, two-handed, cast-and-retrieve routine that defines muskie fishing.

Ray introduced me to muskie fishing during a recent visit to his boat (make that luxury liner) docked on an Ontario island. Now 75, he started chasing muskies as a teenager on Wisconsin's famous Chippewa flowage. He discovered Lake of the Woods on his honeymoon and has roamed its island-studded waters for 54 years. Going muskie fishing with Ray was like taking catechism from the Pope.

I liked flogging the muskrat better than walking the dog. Ray started me out with an eight-inch hunk of broom handle painted black with an orange belly and prominent eyes. When you twitched the rod tip, the broom-handle bait swam erratically across the surface. Ray called that "walking the dog." It was a frenetic fishing technique.

"Start reeling the instant your bait hits the water and work it all the way back to the rod tip," Ray advised.

The trick was to keep the floating bait in constant motion, swimming back to the boat. Muskies lose interest in a bait that hesitates, Ray said. If you see a muskie following your bait, you reel faster so it appears to be attempting to get away. The next move is the muskie's.

"Sometimes they just nudge the bait and sometimes the water explodes," said Ray.

The explosive attack is the rare moment that motivates muskie anglers. A muskie may be more than four feet in length and weigh upwards of 30 pounds. Angling encounters are always memorable, but infrequent. Known as the Fish of 10,000 Casts, muskies must be coaxed into striking.

The first day was spent casting—and casting some more. Ray's friend Don Rasmussen of Baudette operated the boat and successfully jigged for walleyes while I stood in the bow, unsuccessfully walking the dog and flogging the muskrat over rock piles and weedbeds known to harbor muskies. Once, a small one followed the muskrat back to the boat. When this occurs, you are supposed to use the rod tip to trace a figure eight with the bait and excite the follower into striking. But the excitement was all mine and I flubbed the maneuver.

The next day I fished with Ray, who hurtled through the maze of islands at full throttle—no small feat in a lake where innumerable boulders lurk beneath the surface. We motored from one muskie hideout to another, looking for active fish. Ray was throwing something that skittered across the surface like a duckling. On his advice, I stuck with the muskrat.

"More muskies are caught on bucktails than anything else," he said. "Any color works, as long as it's black."

Muskie fishing requires physical and mental concentration. Casting and retrieving with a stout rod and a level-wind reel is a full body workout. Wearing polarized sunglasses, you intently watch the bait and look for approaching fish. Though it may be hours before a muskie appears, you must remain ever ready for that moment of truth.

Ray spoke of muskies as individual fish. He talked of a big one caught and released by several anglers, including himself, not far from his boat dock. He told tales of fish landed, ones that got away, and one that never bites at all.

"He lives in that weedbed where you saw the little one yesterday. And he's got eyes like this," said Ray, holding his thumb and forefinger in a silver dollar-sized circle. "Must weigh a hundred pounds."

Though he's often cast to the monster muskie's lair, the fish has never shown interest in his bait. The muskie has another way of making its presence known.

"You get the feeling you're being watched. Look around and there he'll be, lying just beneath the surface," Ray said. "Of course, he'll never bite. He just likes to see who is fishing for him."

I kept flogging the muskrat, but no muskies, monsters or otherwise, went after it. But I didn't get bored. In fact, I wanted to keep casting when it was time to quit. Muskies, they say, trigger obsessive behavior in anglers, and I was exhibiting familiar symptoms.

"I don't know if I should thank you or curse you for introducing me to muskie fishing," I told Ray.

He smiled, knowing the Minnesota population of muskie anglers had just grown by one.

Techno dinosaur
lumbers from the woods

The three-hour power outage was scheduled and announced in the paper. That's what I learned after the power went out in Hovland...but before I e-mailed my weekly stories to Minnesota Outdoor News.

Two hundred and fifty miles away, a deadline loomed menacingly over my fearless editor, Rob. Computer disk in hand, I headed for the Cook County News-Herald office 20 miles away in Grand Marais, where another fearless editor, Steve, had agreed to e-mail my stories. But when I showed up, he laughed at me.

"Where did you find that disk?" Steve asked. "Out in the woods?"

My stories were contained on a 5 1/4-inch floppy disk, but it might as well have been an eight-track tape. The disk was extinct technology. The newspaper no longer had a computer that could accept it.

Editor Steve picked up the phone and began calling around town. Grand Marais is small and remote. You'd think someone other than me would still have a six-year-old computer. Nope. Everyone he called was amazed and amused (mostly amused) that someone still used such ancient technology. It was like writing with a quill pen and parchment.

Finally, we located a machine with a 5 1/4-inch disk drive. Sherry at the accountant's office said they had a relic buried in a storage shed. She even agreed to go get it. Sherry, I knew from previous experience, first sharpened her wit (often using me as a whetstone) while working as a soda jerk in high school. Her skills have greatly improved. She can now say "Gotcha, dummy," with merely a look as she hands you boxes of geriatric computer equipment. I said thank you. You have to be humble when you're technologically impaired.

Steve plugged the components together and fired it up. Windows 3.0—software from another epoch—appeared on the screen. The mouse didn't work. But we inserted my dinosaur disk and, with some fancy keyboard work from Steve, transferred my stories to a standard-sized disk. He then dialed on to the Internet. In moments, my stories disappeared into cyberspace. I anxiously telephoned Minnesota Outdoor News to see if they'd arrived safely. While we'd been frantically searching for a dinosaur computer, the looming deadline slathered and drooled, soaking Fearless Editor Rob in ill humor. Rob had the stories, but he didn't sound happy.

Steve, on the other hand, who'd wasted an hour of his day in the archaeological digs of computerdom, seemed to derive perverse pleasure from my predicament. His wit, in fact, was nearly as sharp as Sherry's. When I suggested covering the 5 1/4-inch disk drive slot on my machine with duct tape, he gave me an incredulous look.

"Oh," he said, "you actually know what duct tape is?"

Sherry said we could keep the ancient computer, demonstrating about as much magnanimity as if she'd just given us a worn-out shoe. Steve looked around the newspaper shop.

"What am I gonna do with it?" he asked, and with Sherry's infectious generosity said, "Why don't you take it?"

He helped me carry it out to the sidewalk. I loaded the artifact into the back of my pickup, which smelled powerfully of spilled molasses (that's another story) and headed home. The old computer rests in my garage. I don't know what to do with it, but that's OK.

I guess one dinosaur deserves another.

Bear hunt or sanity test?

Sometimes, it's easy to get talked into doing crazy things.

Two years ago, I mentioned to my father that it might be interesting to try bear hunting. The next time we talked, he said our bear license lottery applications were filled out and ready to mail. I signed on the dotted line and we sent them off. We entered the lottery again this year and were successful at drawing permits.

Now, although I live in some of Minnesota's best bear country, my philosophy toward bruins has always been live and let live. Stay out of my garage, my garbage and my apple tree, and we'll get along just fine. In fact, it was my father who, years ago, convinced me that bear hunting might not be my cup of tea.

"Think about it," he said. "You generally shoot the bear just before dark. You have to drag it out in the dark and, believe me, bears aren't easy to drag. Then, because it's so warm in early September, you have to skin it out and cut it up the same night. Sounds like a lot of work to me."

So what made him change his mind? Maybe he's losing his mind. Certainly, Vikki is convinced that I've lost mine.

"I want no part of this," my partner in game processing and cooking said. "I'm not helping you cut it up and I'm not eating it."

My father, after getting the license, also backed out of his end of the bargain. His neighbor had offered him an endless supply of restaurant grease for bear bait. A week before baiting was to begin, I learned Dad had dropped the ball. He had no grease—and his neighbor was leaving on an Alaskan vacation.

"What the heck am I going to do with it?" he asked defensively. "I don't want that stuff stinking up my garage."

Presumably, it's OK if it stinks up your son's garage. It is also OK if your son dumpster dives behind the Bluewater Cafe in Grand Marais to get the grease. Looking into the grease dumpster, where food scraps floated in unappetizing splendor, I questioned my own sanity. Did I want to eat an animal that would eat this stuff?

However, it was the molasses that really got me. I stopped at a feed store to buy corn, sunflower seeds, and molasses for bait while on my way to the Twin Cities. Since I didn't have containers to store the molasses, the feed store sold me (at sinful profit) two used plastic jugs. One of them leaked.

On a hot day, molasses has the consistency of roofing tar and an overpowering, sickeningly sweet odor. It is always hot in the Twin Cities in August. When I parked on an incline, molasses oozed under my tailgate and flowed across the parking lot in a sticky rivulet.

"You'll probably have raccoons stuck to the pavement behind your truck," observed Minnesota Outdoor News editor Rob Drieslein.

Funny guy.

When I got home, I tried to clean out my pickup using the power-spray at the local car wash. That tactic was marginally effective. A couple of days later, I rinsed out the bed with endless buckets of water at a Lake Superior boat launch. That was better, but it was still a little sticky back there.

I'd darned near had enough of bear baiting before ever dumping anything in the woods. But when the baiting period began, I headed out confident that luring bears would be easy in this berry-poor year. At five selected stumps—each located within bait-lugging distance of a backroad—I put out piles of whole corn mixed with molasses and sunflower seeds mixed with grease, confident the bears would soon find them.

Several days later, I decided that baiting bears isn't quite so easy as baiting opponents believe. My five baits were uneaten. A second discovery was that I really enjoyed spending a couple of hours every day roaming in the August woods. As a neophyte baiter, my only theory about the lack of activity was that unusually hot weather slowed bear movements.

Eventually, the weather broke, and a bear found one of my baits. The next day, other bears found three more. I abandoned the unproductive—and most distant—fifth bait a few days later. Now I go out every afternoon to feed the bears. Some seem to prefer the corn and molasses. Others go for the grease. At one site, never so much as a kernel of corn is left. All that remains are large piles of "sign." Dad will probably get that bait.

I hope he shoots a bear when the season opens. As for myself, I'm holding out for one that is extra-large, cinnamon-colored or, preferably, both. Such a beast is only slightly more common than a polar bear on the North Shore. If Dad or I shoot a bear, what will we do with it? Well, we'll home-process the meat and get the hide tanned. If we don't care for the meat, certainly there are plenty of folks who enjoy eating bear in Hovland.

Nevertheless, I can't help but remember my father's words of wisdom about all the hot, hard work that begins when you pull the trigger. When a bear arrives, don't be surprised if this hunter puts the crosshairs on its shoulder and then quietly says, "Bang."

Blowdown brook trout

"Can I help you?" asked the young woman in the Forest Service uniform.

I was crouched beside the wall map in the Tofte District office, trying to find a place to go fishing. It was a specific place, supposedly populated with brook trout—a location I wasn't inclined to share. But the map wasn't quite accurate and the woman didn't look like the brookie type. I took a chance.

Pointing to my destination, I asked if she knew the whereabouts of an old road the map didn't show. She didn't. The old road let you drive closer to where a cold creek joined a big river, the kind of place where brook trout hang out in August. On this map, reaching that junction from the nearest road required a long walk.

"The map was updated last year," the woman offered.

"Oh well," I replied, "I'm not worried about getting lost."

Endless summer rains have our North Shore rivers running full and inspired me to an August fly-fishing jag. On previous evenings I'd spent an hour or so poking about in the lower reaches of some rivers near home, not catching much but thoroughly enjoying the fishing.

In August, even when the rivers are up, the odds of catching a lake-run trout or salmon are low. Although landing a coaster brook trout, errant steelhead or a king salmon was possible, my real reason for being there was to wade familiar waters and stretch my casting arm. Three evenings of fishing turned up two seven-inch rainbow trout and three smallmouth bass.

Tonight I was going inland to check out a place I'd long heard about, but never fished. My first goal was to find the old road and save some walking on a hot afternoon. A few miles of driving turned up no shortcuts. I parked at a culvert where the new road crossed the creek. The map details were sketchy, but the mouth of the creek appeared to be at least a mile downstream. On went the waders, over the shoulder went a tackle bag, and—fly rod in hand—I was off. The time was roughly 5:45 p.m. I left a bottle of Gatorade in the truck—no sense carrying the extra weight.

This creek, like so many others, meanders through nearly impenetrable tag alder bottoms. I stuck to higher ground on the south bank, within earshot of the stream, where the going was easier among the spruce and jackpine. Easier...but not easy. The Fourth of July storm that had flattened forests in the Boundary Waters had passed through here, too. Every so often I detoured around fresh blowdowns. I hadn't gone very far before it became evident this would be a long walk. Perhaps those with lesser heart or greater brains would've turned back then, but I had a destination. Blowdowns, knee-deep muck, and the rising temperature inside my waders weren't stopping me.

The storm damage was patchy. I'd walk for a while without seeing blowdowns, then find the way blocked by a line of twisted and broken trees. The only way forward was to climb over or go around. In one place, where spruces tumbled into a tag alder thicket, trying to get through was like grappling with a living, green wall. Eventually, I reached the old road where—surprise, surprise— someone had sawed passage through the windfalls. There were tire tracks. Doors slammed.

It's odd to encounter someone driving a sedan in a place you walked through hell to reach. The man and his young son were friendly. Fishing could've been worse, he said, the blowdowns could've been better. He told me where the old road met the new road. I resolved to walk out that way, though it was longer, to avoid renegotiating hell at dusk.

My destination was now within striking distance, but what a hike. Now on the north bank, I encountered places where new blowdowns were crisscrossed over balsams killed by spruce budworms a few years ago. This blowdown-on-blowdown stuff was really fun. Every so often I paused to listen for the murmur of the big river. Finally, I heard it. Minutes later, I pushed through the tag alders to the strong-running stream. The fabled junction pool was below a short rapids. It was nearly 7 p.m.

Reaching the pool, I knelt down and drank several handfuls of water. Perhaps Giardia would strike tomorrow, but it beat dying of thirst tonight. My wader-wrapped, overheated body was soaking with sweat, my eyeglasses were opaque with steam. Rain began to sprinkle. The mosquitoes found me. A dose of bug dope stung like aftershave, but it kept the insects at bay. My shirt was soaked, so I couldn't wipe off my eyeglasses. Sans specs, I squinted to string up the fly rod. Still squinting, I tied on a black Whiskey Fly.

The creek slid into the river at the head of the pool, forming a cold, foam-flecked eddy beside the main current. Standing on a grassy tussock where the currents met, I cast into the creek flow. On the second cast, a solid thump broke the light tippet. Still soaked and steamy, I cut the tapered leader back to a heavier weight and tied on another Whiskey Fly, wondering why anyone goes trout fishing. Two casts later, I had my answer, delivered by a swirling strike and quick run to midstream.

In fishing, "big" is a relative term. Tarpon anglers, for instance, seek man-sized fish. You can catch northern pike as long as your leg. But on a North Shore trout stream, a foot-long brookie is "big." The one on the end of my line easily made the grade. The trout ran and tussled. When it tired, I drew the fish near. I was reaching for it when the Whiskey Fly popped free and imbedded itself in the crook between my right thumb and forefinger.

The pooped-out brookie was laying in some flooded grass. In a moment, it would certainly disappear with a quick kick. I tried to pull out the fly and grab the fish. No go. The hook was buried beyond the barb. Moments like this require calm, deliberate thinking. I dug into my tackle bag, found a pair of scissors and snipped the leader at the fly. Then I put the scissors away, reached down, and picked up the trout with my left hand. It was fat in my grip.

Stowing the trout in the tackle bag, I returned to the problem at hand...rather, in my hand. Passing line inside the hook bend and pulling back, standard fishing first aid, didn't work because of the fly's awkward location. Hoping a quick yank with a pair of pliers wasn't necessary, I pushed down on the butt of the fly and worked it back and forth. Painlessly, the hook slid free. It was nearly 7:15.

I made a few more casts with the Whiskey Fly, missed a half-hearted strike, and changed to a squirrel-tail streamer. I pulled it through the creek current a couple of times and then worked the main flow, roll casting to reach the far side. A trout took with a splash as the fly drifted downstream. This one was almost long enough to be called "big." Dinner for two was in the bag.

They stopped biting, but it was time to start hiking, anyway. I decided to fish my way up the creek. I crossed to the south bank, moved away from the water to detour some alders and never made it back to the stream. I battled blowdowns all the way back to the old road. After several handfuls of water and a couple of quick casts in a pool below the culvert, I started hiking. It was about 8 p.m. Following the old road out to the new road, I was gulping Gatorade at the truck by 8:45.

I took off my waders, then my shirt, and stood hot, soaked, and wobbly in the dusk. All told, I'd spent perhaps 20 minutes actually fishing. I smiled. By a trout fisherman's measure, the day was a success.

Hot, electric night

It is rare when this North Shore angler thinks the weather is too hot to go fishing.

In recent days, the thermometer located on the shady side of the garage climbed beyond 90 degrees every afternoon. I had free time in the evenings, and a fishing itch that needed scratching, but the heat sapped my motivation. Just thinking about the task of loading the canoe and fishing gear, much less putting in the effort necessary to reach some out-of-the-way fishing hole, made me sweat.

So I stayed home and, like a lizard, kept motions to a minimum. We don't have air conditioning, because we rely on Lake Superior to keep us cool. This heat wave was bigger than the lake—and that's saying something. The dogs fared better than me. Abby spent the days outside, lying in the cool, shaded grass. Casey stayed indoors, never far from a fan. He must have a leak-proof bladder, because he refused to go outside until the sun dipped below the trees.

That's about the time Vikki arrives home from work. She spends eight hours in a retail store dealing with the sweaty, shuffling mass of humanity we call tourists. The dogs and I give her lots of space. The other night the house was so warm we didn't feel like making dinner. Instead we decided to drive up to Ryden's Café on the Canadian border. Going for a drive wasn't as good as going fishing, but it was a suitable antidote for heat-inspired stir-craziness.

The drive along Highway 61 through Grand Portage Indian Reservation is outstanding, whether the temperature is 90 above or 20 below. On this evening, Lake Superior was rippled by a northwest breeze that blew the warm surface water off-shore. As a result, the lake's water temperature was likely in the 40s. Where the hot, humid air met the cold lake, a fog formed. From the highway, it looked like a soft layer of mist over the blue-gray water. If you were in a boat, likely you could look up and see the sky, but your immediate surroundings would be obscured by the fog.

Dinner was good. While we were eating, dark clouds came over the ridges, bringing an early twilight with them. We started home under an ominous sky. The clouds were the color of a fresh bruise. I was happy to be sitting in an air-conditioned truck, rather than bobbing around on some pond in my canoe. That feeling was reinforced when a spectacular bolt of lightning stabbed the lake.

It was the first of many. As we drove we were treated to a fantastic lightning display over Lake Superior. Sometimes, there was a pulsing, electric flash in the atmosphere. Others were massive, jagged bolts hurling from the clouds to the lake. We said "Wow!" more than once.

As we arrived home, the sky was breaking up to the west. The sun, although not visible, bathed the world in an eerie, rosy glow. I parked the truck in the driveway and took a slow walk across the yard. Thunder rumbled, lightning flashed, and a few half-hearted raindrops fell. The air was charged with electricity.

Perhaps just being outdoors was a little risky, but I was drawn to the sky. The clouds were broken. Some were stuffy and dark; others frivolous wisps. Curtains of rain crossed through the atmosphere, but didn't seem to reach the ground. What color were the clouds now? Pink? Magenta? I decided it was a color for which I had no name. It is rare when this writer is at a loss for a word. I went inside then, humbled by the beauty of a hot summer night.

The Irishmen

There was an unfamiliar motor home in the driveway and a knock on the door. An older man in a green waxed cotton jacket was standing on the stoop when I opened the door.

"They sent me here from the Post Office," he said in greeting. "I was told you know something about the local fly-fishing."

Things like this happen in small towns during tourist season. We talked for a moment and I invited him in. He was an Irishman from Massachusetts, driving and fishing his way to Alaska with a recently retired friend from Ireland. Pretty soon Brandon and his friend Alton were sitting at the kitchen table, talking about fishing, German shepherds (Brandon's dog, Tara, was traveling with them), wing shooting, and what not.

They were particularly interested in my late Grandpa Casey's collection of Irish books. Alton had read one, an account of growing up on a remote island off the Irish coast, in the original Gaelic. The pair were staying in Hovland through the holiday weekend, waiting for a fishing rod Brandon had forwarded to the Post Office. On a whim I invited them to go fishing that evening, and to celebrate Independence Day with us, some friends, and grilled moose steaks the next day. They went to five o'clock Mass in Grand Marais and were supposed to

93

show up at my house afterward. I was ready at six. They didn't make it until seven.

"Lots of nice people at that church," Brandon said.

"We couldn't get away," remarked Alton.

We went to a lake where the mayflies were hatching and 12-inch rainbow trout were rising like popcorn. Brandon, who spends his autumns fishing for salmon on Nova Scotia's Margaree River, was an accomplished fly-fisher. Alton, on the other hand, was all thumbs with a spinning rod.

I gave him a little green floating Rapala, which looked enough like a mayfly to satisfy the trout. In fact, he'd often have several strikes on the same cast. The trout were safe, though, because the concepts of setting the hook, holding the rod tip up when playing a fish, and even turning the reel crank in the right direction were somewhat beyond Alton's grasp. But he didn't seem to mind. The trout that Brandon hooked danced like Fourth of July skyrockets.

"Oh laddie!" Brandon would say each time a rainbow went aerial. "Oh laddie!"

He talked about dapping for trout on lakes in Ireland. To dap, the Irish use a very long rod and fish with four dry flies. The line is held out of the water and has a length of floss attached like a pennant. The floss catches the breeze and skitters the flies across the surface. Brandon said the trout are attracted to the motion of the flies.

"I think it would work here, too," he said.

He also talked of shooting ducks and pheasants for market while growing up in rural Ireland. Poaching was a way of life. Shooting pheasants from a tree outside the gamekeeper's house sounded, well, sporting. Brandon said he was chased many times, but never caught. He hasn't hunted since he was 23.

At dinner the next evening, he peppered me and my friends with questions. He learned everything he could about sled dogs, trapping, public land, wolves, black bears, and north-woods life. All agreed he and Alton told some marvelous stories in return. Now, I don't invite every strange fisherman that knocks on my door to dinner. But I do occasionally act on impulse. Maybe it's the luck of the Irish, but that spontaneity pays some great dividends.

Fishing with Cleopatra

The other day, my friend Dan Parkinson of Superior, Wisconsin, and my father, Dan Perich of Duluth, came up to my house in Hovland to go fishing. Parkinson and I grew up together, and the three of us have shared many fishing trips. But it was nearly 10 years since we'd last fished together—you know how it goes.

We paddled and portaged into a BWCAW lake to fish for smallmouth bass; three of us in a 17-foot canoe. My father had first brought us into the canoe country back in the days when you could use an outboard motor to reach lakes such as this. Mr. Parkinson and I paddled, while my father sat in the middle like some bald and grizzled Cleopatra. While we paddled, he told stories—all of which we'd heard before. But we didn't mind hearing them again.

Fishing three from a canoe was easier than you might think. The bass were available, but not eager. You had to bounce them on the nose with a jig and twister. Dan seemed to be catching the most fish, but Dad's were adding up faster. Dad said he'd caught a dozen, although Dan and I could only recall seeing him boat three or four fish. Pretty soon Cleopatra said it was time for lunch. Dan and I kept fishing, but a steady barrage of complaints issued from the center of the canoe. We heard about how uncomfortable the middle seat was and how long it had been since breakfast. We went to shore.

By this time, it was late afternoon. Dan wanted to be on the road back to Duluth before dark. This left us only a couple of hours to fish. We decided to let the wind drift us back down the shoreline a mile or so to the portage. Our plan was put on hold when I saw the first muskie. I was looking down into 10 feet of water when we passed over a muskie as long as my leg. A few minutes later, Dan got the same fish to take a look at a four-inch plastic worm. Then we saw another muskie. And another. I knew it would be dark before we got back to the truck.

We were undergunned with ultralight tackle, but Dad hooked an unseen fish that made a few strong runs and eventually broke him off. The bass fishing improved as evening approached, although many of the fish we caught coughed up gobs of partially digested minnows. Occasionally, we saw bass chasing minnows on the surface. Just before sunset the lake became still. I yodeled at two nearby loons and they answered me. Would you believe my companions joked about this masterful demonstration of woodcraft? They'd probably still be cracking loon jokes if we hadn't seen slashing swirls of large fish out in the middle of the lake. Even though we were just a long cast from the portage, we paddled out to see what was causing the commotion.

What we found was a school of minnows several acres in size. I don't think I've encountered anything quite like that before. Big fish—probably smallmouth and whitefish—ripped through the minnows like feeding sharks. Try as we might, we couldn't catch them. Finally, approaching darkness brought an end to our frustration. We crossed the portage while it was barely light enough to see, then paddled hard to cover the remaining three miles in the dark. Dan and Dad had a three-hour drive home, and Dan had to go to work in the morning. As we approached the landing, Cleopatra piped up.

"You two are getting pretty good at paddling," he said. "Maybe next year I'll teach you how to run the motor."

A salmon parable

The next time it rains, I may wander down to the river. I've heard reports that Lake Superior trollers have had unusually good fishing for salmon. Now that September is here, perhaps a few Chinooks will head up the rivers to spawn. It's been six years since I last caught a river Chinook. Casey, my yellow Lab, was then a rabbit-sized pup. I'd stopped to make a few drifts in the Poplar River at Lutsen Resort and stung a salmon—a big one—in the pool beneath the waterfall. We battled there for a while, with Casey tied by his leash on the bank, then the salmon made a run for the lake. I followed.

A Chinook salmon is like a locomotive with fins. I held on while this one made for Michigan and asked a passing tourist to fetch my pup. He did. The epic struggle between man and fish was complicated by the fact that I was using six-pound-test line. Suffice to say that the battle lasted long enough to draw a sizeable audience from the resort. Eventually, I slipped my hand around the base of the salmon's tail. It was lake-bright and heavy—over 20 pounds. It was also hooked just outside the mouth on the tip of the chin. In my book, that's a foul-hooked—and illegal to keep—fish. My audience didn't know that. When I released the salmon, they applauded.

That was the grand finale of a rabid decade of salmon fish-

ing. During the 1980s, I spent so much time chasing Chinooks every autumn that occasionally I woke myself by setting the hook in my dreams. You might say I was sal-manic. So were most of my male friends and co-workers. It was easy to get that way when you tangled with a dozen 10- to 20-pound fish in a morning of fishing. Although Minnesota began stocking Pacific salmon in Lake Superior in the late sixties, it wasn't until the early eighties that the fishery took off. Then, for a decade, it was Katie-bar-the-door. Every autumn, North Shore rivers swarmed with big fish.

The salmon runs created a stir of excitement. In fact, I don't think it's a stretch to say that salmon fishing helped kick-start the North Shore's tourist boom. Tettegouche, Temperance River, and Cascade River state parks were packed with anglers and people who were watching the action. "Stock more salmon!" became a rallying cry for tourism promoters. However, in the icy waters of Lake Superior, it wasn't natural for a fish to grow to 20 pounds in just four years—the length of a Chinook's life cycle. The salmon and a recovering population of native lake trout preyed heavily upon the smelt—a prolific bait fish which had drawn an earlier generation of dipnet-wielding tourists to the Shore every spring. The spring smelt runs declined and so did the autumn salmon runs.

Neither smelt nor salmon have disappeared from Lake Superior, but both are far less common than they were during the 1980s. Biologists say that lake trout and one of their natural prey, herring, have increased to take their place. Returns on salmon stockings have been so low that Minnesota has considered dropping the program. Former sal-maniacs like myself found other things to do. The tourism industry rolled on without us, and now shoppers and strollers far outnumber anglers along the North Shore. A couple of years ago, a former fishing friend called prior to making an autumn excursion with his family along the Shore. He asked, wistfully, about the fishing. I asked if he planned to wet a line.

"No," he said. "We'll just tie sweaters around our necks like all the other tourists, take a short walk, and sigh over how beautiful it is in the Great Outdoors."

My friend had changed, but so have the times. The North Shore, like so many wild places, is becoming no more than a scenic backdrop for an overpriced vacation or a snooty address for a second home. Folks who have come here for years to fish, hunt, camp, or canoe scratch their heads and marvel at how much development has occurred since their last visit. Increasingly, we are replacing what is natural with something artificial. I guess the Chinooks were part of that. We created a fishery that seemed, even at the time, too good to be true. And it was.

Sometimes, a new arrival finds a niche and becomes, as biologists say, "naturalized." Here on the North Shore, Norwegians and steelhead are good examples of that. But other things are popular or profitable for a time and then run their course. Right now, North Shore cash registers jingle merrily as tourists and urban immigrants roll in. Times are good. Maybe I'm a pessimist. Or maybe growing up in northern Minnesota has taught me that this place has its ups and downs. Anyhow, I can't help but wonder, what will be the next salmon on the North Shore?

Alone on the lake and free

The breeze was from the southwest when I motored out of the bay Saturday morning. Choppy waves were starting to cap and it looked unruly offshore. A freighter that passed as I launched the boat was already nearly out of sight on Lake Superior's tumbled horizon. The wind moved the boat around while I set the downrigger line—a two-handed operation that required steering the outboard tiller with my knee. It was early and the breeze was likely to build, so I curbed a desire to explore far places and planned a troll that kept me within a couple of miles of the launch. I had no need for adventure.

Once my two lines were in the water, I settled into fishing, which, on the big lake, means running the motor at trolling speed. An easy task, to be sure, but on Superior you never let your attention waver from the business at hand. I scanned the sky, wondering if the high, green hills of the North Shore were hiding any weather. That's when I noticed the fighter jet contrails 30,000 feet above the Canadian border.

Even here, alone on the world's largest lake, it was impossible to get away from the terrible events of the past week. At home, the television showed incessant images of the September 11 terrorist attacks and their aftermath in New York and Washington, D.C. I was out here in part to get away from that, but there was no getting away. To the best of my knowledge, no one I know was killed in the attacks or subsequent rescue. Still, it is impossible not to take this incident personally. We are shocked by this attack on American soil and numbed by the immediacy of television. Out on the lake, away from all of that, I thought about things.

My only brush with terrorism occurred 20 years ago when a friend and I shared a car on a night train from Edinburgh to London with members of the Scot Royal Guard—the soldiers with the big, furry hats who guard Buckingham Palace—who were coming back after Christmas furlough. We drank some beers and made some friends. Months later, back in the USA, I heard the Royal Guard was bombed by Irish terrorists and many were killed. Out on the lake, I thought about those kids, dead now longer than they'd been alive.

I thought, too, about a black, September night four years ago when a fellow Hovland fire fighter was buried beneath rubble when a two-story chimney collapsed. The footage of the collapsing World Trade Center was eerily similar. Our friend, though now paralyzed, beat all odds and survived. Nevertheless, none of us who were there will forget the darkness of that night. I know how the New York fire fighters who are searching for their fallen comrades feel.

These were heavy thoughts, to be sure, for a morning of fishing.

But I can't say they were thoughts of despair or hopelessness. Instead I was happy to be alive and on the water. Sometimes, it is the simplest things that we treasure most. Out on the lake, I felt very free. I thought about a friend and former neighbor who recently came for a visit. During World War II, he had spent four years as a Japanese prisoner of war. Enduring unimaginable horror and privation, he survived—at tremendous cost to his physical and emotional health. I am humbled by the price he paid for my freedom.

We live in a free nation. We can say what we think, go where we choose, marry whom we love, practice our religious faiths, and be rewarded for hard work. We have lots to eat, places to live, and time to enjoy our friends and families. As a people, we can hardly ask for more. The tragedy of the recent attacks reminds us that freedom cannot be taken for granted. Defense of freedom defines American history. Looking ahead, there's rough water on the nation's horizon. I hope that as free people, we have the courage to seek justice rather than revenge.

Out on the lake, that's what I was thinking.

Out in the Popples

Casey and me

Recently, friends have said I ought to write a book—about my dog.

"Why don't you do a funny, Patrick McManus-style, book about Casey?" they ask.

The only problem is that right now, in the middle of bird season, I can't see anything funny about that rock-headed yellow Lab. In fact, I have trouble saying his name without adding a long string of expletives. Casey hears those words so often that he answers to them as well as his own name. As my Dad observed on a recent hunt, Casey just isn't a team player. He has the drive and natural abilities of a champion, and will hold his own with any dog when it comes to rousting pheasants from tangled cover or finding downed ducks in a sea of bulrushes, but he has a few bad habits.

For instance, you don't leave ducks lying about in the duck blind when Casey is around. He'll sneak off with one if he gets the chance. A couple of weeks ago, he ate an entire green-winged teal, swallowing it whole, then climbed in his kennel for a long ride home from North Dakota without any noticeable ill effects. He also gobbles up the grouse guts (and feet, feathers and heads) left behind by thoughtless folks who clean their birds at boat landings and similar places.

The worse the guts smell, the better. He eats other things, too, but we'll spare the details.

In the duck marsh, Casey adds new meaning to the phrase "jump-shooting." You really haven't canoed until you've paddled alone in the dark with a 70-pound Lab poised like a high-diver on the bow plate. I bought pontoons for my canoe after taking an unexpected swim on the opening day of duck season last year—and several times this season I've thanked my lucky stars for that purchase. The other day, Dad and I were so fed up with Casey's leaps from the canoe every time we flushed ducks that we made him swim a half-mile upstream in a weedy channel in a vain effort to tire him out. He wasn't even breathing hard when he eventually climbed back into the canoe.

Fortunately, this bird-eating, muscle-bound brute is a lover, not a fighter. Our first grouse hunt of the year was cut short a quarter mile from home when Casey got beat up by a small sled dog with a bad disposition. However, despite a certain operation, he still takes that lover stuff a little too far. A friend of mine, trying to discourage Casey's affection, once said, "It looks like he likes my leg better than yours."

Maybe a pro trainer could help my problem pup, but I'm not planning to send Casey to doggie boot camp. As a hunting dog, he falls short of perfection, but as a hunter, so do I. Together though, we make a pretty good team. He misses a few commands—and I miss a few easy shots—but we get our birds. When I returned from a recent hunting trip (minus one green-winged teal), a friend asked me how it went with Casey.

"Oh, the usual," I said, "some good and some bad."

"Well, that's what I'd expect," my friend replied, "because I've hunted with both of you."

Not hobbits

One of my friends vividly describes some northwoods fishing trips he's made with his father in just a few words. "Sometimes," Pete says, "the day was a success if we found the lake."

Anyone who's spent time beating the brush has been on similar excursions. At the end of the day you're cold, wet and dragging everything but a heavy game bag. These jaunts begin innocently enough. For instance, on a recent afternoon, Vikki and I walked a path for partridge with our yellow Lab, Casey. The trail we took leads to the top of a bluff with a sweeping vista of Minnesota and Ontario. Call it hunting with a view.

The sun was sinking when we reached the top, but we had nearly an hour of daylight left to walk the mile or so back to our parked truck. Unwilling to trudge the same path twice, I suggested that we continue on the trail over the bluff and cut through the woods on the other side to reach the logging road where our truck was parked. It was about the same distance, I told Vikki, so she agreed.

As we descended the far side of the bluff, it became apparent that most sightseers hike to the top and then turn around and go back. The trail was somewhat overgrown and blocked by balsam deadfalls—the rotting victims of a spruce budworm

111

plague. Vikki, whose shorter legs take two steps to my one, soon fell behind. Dusk arrived. The deadfalls became more numerous. When darkness fell, our way was so clogged that not even Casey could find the trail. Soon we were picking our way through tangles we could barely see. "We don't have far to go," I assured Vikki. Of course, we didn't have a flashlight.

Since I knew where we were, becoming lost wasn't part of the equation. However, we had to negotiate several hundred yards of fallen trees. Although I could step or climb over most of them, every horizontal balsam was a hurdle for Vikki. And, if we became separated by more than 50 feet, she couldn't see me. "Pretend you're a hobbit," I said, hoping to appeal to her love of fantasy novels. I can't print her reply.

The only way to walk in the woods at night is to go at your own pace and trust your feet. That's what we did. Occasionally, we'd get 30 or 40 feet of tangle-free travel. Then a chest-high blowdown would force us to detour. Every now and then, one of us fell down. Eventually, we stepped out on the rutted logging road, which seemed as wide as an interstate highway. Since we were still some distance from the truck, I stepped lively to go get it and save Vikki the walk. Casey went with me.

The night was dark. Overhead, I could see just one evening star and some spectral clouds. We were alone in the midst of wild, uninhabited country. There was no sound of distant traffic, no glow from far-off lights. Trusting my feet to find the rocks and ruts in the road, I hit my nighttime stride. The deadfall hell was behind us. Soon we'd be sitting down to a late but well-deserved supper. I savored the silent darkness, thinking about this time and many others when my path as a hunter led to unexpected adventure. It felt so good to be out there, walking on a beautiful night, that I reached the truck before realizing something.

We hadn't flushed a grouse.

B Team pup makes varsity

The grouse season got off to a very uneven start when disastrous calamity and—to a far lesser degree—rainy weather kept me out of the woods on opening day. On Sunday, clearing skies gave me a chance to clear my head with a long walk along the Canadian border with Casey, my vacuum-nosed, bird-eating, yellow Lab, and Abby, our year-old German shepherd. The dogs flushed plenty of birds and we left the woods with a plump game bag. On the final couple of miles, Casey trotted beside me like a genteel country squire, displaying an uncharacteristic lack of vigor I attributed to a tiring first hunt.

Wrong. That evening, Vikki discovered an inch-and-a-half gash on the inside of Casey's right hind leg, which likely occurred as he porpoised across a quarter mile of balsam blowdown, where sharp-broken branches stuck out like punji sticks. The next day Dr. Kim, the Grand Marais vet, advised stitches and 10 days of rest. Poor Casey was out of commission before he even ate a partridge. And poor me. A certain friend and I have a little rivalry over who can put the most grouse on the table. It may lack the prestige of the National Grouse and Woodcock Hunt, but we take our competition seriously. She has a darned good dog and hunts every day. My situation looked bleak.

The next afternoon, Abby and I took an after-work walk through our home coverts. My fingers were crossed, because she'd shown some interest in hunting while out with Casey. Maybe this B Team pup would rise to the occasion. Short on style but long on enthusiasm, Abby quartered along the edge of a huge tag alder thicket. In a quarter mile, she flushed two woodcock. Things were looking up.

The afternoon's first grouse thundered out of a stand of young popple—off Abby's nose. I began to "read" her and know when she was birdy with hot scent. Not long afterward, I learned her nose wasn't discriminating. She got excited in a tangle of hazel brush. I paused and waited for a flush that never occurred. Walking up, I found her focused on a hollow log. Abby's quarry, apparently, was a chipmunk. Nevertheless, she flushed another grouse that evening. The next time out, Abby put up a grouse that I was able to shoot. She didn't retrieve it, but she did stand over the downed bird. At least she didn't eat it. She became birdy—or maybe chipmunky—a couple more times that evening, but we didn't flush any more grouse. But I don't think we walked past any birds, either.

It feels strange following a German shepherd through the grouse woods. Casey may have some faults, but he hunts hard and looks good doing it. Walking behind a yellow Lab, even if you have to occasionally wrestle a bird away from him, you at least feel like an honest-to-goodness bird hunter. Abby and I, on the other hand, are decidedly bush league. Amazingly, she's quickly learned the game. Since the first day we entered the woods with a shotgun, she seemed to understand that our daily walks now had a purpose. Perhaps she noticed a change in Casey's demeanor that day, especially when he flushed a grouse and I shot at it. She had probably learned the rudiments of hunting by following Casey as he flushed dozens of grouse during our walks of the past year.

Whatever. I'm less inclined to contemplate the mysteries of dogs than to enjoy the rewards of their kinship. While Casey mends, Abby and I are working as a team. And we are maintaining a narrow lead over our competition. My confidence in

Abby's abilities is growing. Yesterday, she put up a bird in a chest-high tangle of wild rose and moose-browsed hazel brush. I took a quick shot as it sailed into some young popples. Following up, the grouse flushed from a tree and sailed down-hill. I shot, but was unable to see if the bird fell.

A dog that hunts to the command "dead bird" will put a sur-prising number of grouse in your game bag in situations like this. Abby doesn't know that command. So we walked over to where I'd last seen the bird to see if it would flush again—con-firming a miss. The bird's flight path led us into a mess of bal-sam blowdown. If the grouse was down, it was unlikely that I would find it. But Abby has a much better nose than me. In moments, she found the grouse.

She was praised and praised again. Her hunting partner's head swelled. Within two hundred yards she became birdy again. Hot on the scent, she zigzagged through the cover like a pro. Her course led to a fallen log. A chipmunk scampered down the log and scurried through the brush. Abby stayed on its trail for another 25 yards. Oh well, she's just a pup. And she flushed two more grouse just a few minutes later. After all, the B Team is where the young and inexperienced learn to play the game.

Hopefully, Casey will be back on the varsity squad by the duck opener. Abby, who just learned how to swim two weeks ago, isn't ready for the marsh. And, as Vikki keeps reminding me, Abby is supposed to be her companion when Casey and I are off hunting. So Abby will return to the B Team and she may sit out a few hunts. But I suspect it will be impossible to keep this hunting German shepherd down.

116

The cat in the road

Jack Frost finally breathed a chill into the bland, warm weather that defined September. At night, bright northern lights danced and shimmered overhead. At sunrise, ice crystals sparkled on our frosty lawn. Aspen and birch suddenly blazed golden with surreal brilliance. I took a late-afternoon hike down an old logging road to bask in the autumnal glow. The trail passes through acres of aspen thickets seldom hunted by anyone but me. Carrying a shotgun and accompanied by two dogs, I hoped to flush a grouse or two. But the hunting was secondary to enjoying the view. High ridges rose like amber mountains from the surrounding forest. Few places are more beautiful at this time of year.

I got back to the truck at sunset, grouse-less, but satisfied with the stroll. I loaded up two tired but happy dogs and started driving home. Cresting a rise on the Arrowhead Trail, I saw a dark-colored animal standing on the road some distance ahead of me. The critter was about fox-sized, but was taller and lacked a long, bushy tail. As I approached, it walked off the road. So I sped up, hoping to catch another, closer look before it vanished in the woods.

I did. Standing just a few feet off the gravel was a wild cat with tufted ears, furry feet, and a black-tipped tail—a lynx.

Although I've happened upon lynx tracks on occasion, this was my first up-close-and-personal encounter with one. The lynx looked at me, then turned and started walking away. I rolled down the window and whistled, with no effect on the lynx. Then I squeaked like a mouse. The animal stopped and turned to look at me. Reaching behind the seat, I found my camera case and started fumbling with it to fish out the camera while watching the lynx. It started walking and I again stopped it with a squeak. Just as I got the camera out of the bag, the cat took a few more steps and disappeared.

Rebel's gift

Bringing home a goose and a gadwall wasn't good enough.

"I want a couple of grouse for dinner," Vikki said.

Shrugging, I loaded Casey and Abby in the pickup and left for the woods. The destination came to mind on the way: Rebel's Grave. It's my name for a stand of young aspen that's usually good for a bird or two. Our late yellow Lab, Rebel, retrieved his first grouse in there. Five years ago, Vikki and I tearfully buried him nearby. A bear dug up the grave the next spring, but I always pause at the hole in the ground beneath the aspen with REBEL carved in the bark. Today the dogs stood beside me.

"Get us some birds, Reb," I quietly said.

The aspens are bordered by a cedar and spruce swamp. I followed a skid trail kept passable by moose for a half mile or so to some dry beaver ponds. From more than a decade of past hunts I knew where the birds are most likely to flush. None got up for a quarter mile. The first one thundered out from a low tangle near a cedar-shrouded spring. I never saw it and couldn't flush it again. We walked all the way to the ponds without seeing another. On a whim, I turned east and found a moose trail going my way.

The trail traversed high ground along the swamp edge, wending through a balsam blowdown mess growing back in hazel brush and aspen. It looked like a great winter browsing area for moose. No doubt that's why the big moose antler, shed last winter, was lying on the edge of the trail. When I stooped to pick it up, the dogs flushed a bird in the hazel brush. A quick shot put the grouse in the bag.

The antler was dropped last winter and hadn't been chewed by bears or rodents. Hoping the bull moose had dropped his other antler nearby, I looked around. A short distance away, I found two more large antlers lying about four feet apart. They, too, had been shed last winter. Any day is good when you find a moose antler. Finding three large ones (they measure 25, 33 and 34 inches from base to tip) in an area not much larger than your living room is an amazing stroke of luck. I piled them up to carry out later and continued hunting. One more partridge would make dinner.

The going got tough. We humped through the blowdown and followed a tiny creek downstream to a beaver pond. Then we circled back. Casey became birdy in the hazel brush. Head down and tail thumping, he wove through the thicket until a grouse went skyward. Another shot and we had dinner for two. Now it was time to work up an appetite. A normal, two-armed human being cannot easily carry three heavy moose antlers and a shotgun along a brushy trail. It's a matter of physical logistics. You can lay the antlers across your arms and then hold the gun in a way you hope will keep it from getting scratched. This means you grasp the wrist-thick bases of the antlers with one hand and balance the load on your opposing forearm. As you walk, the brush reaches out with twiggy fingers and tries to pull everything away from you. Stepping over fallen logs is an exquisite balancing act. Frequently, you are forced to pause and adjust your unwieldy load. Before long your arms feel stretched and ready to fall off.

At the spring, the dogs flushed another grouse that whirred across the trail. Welcoming the break, I put down the antlers and followed up. The bird hadn't flown far, but the dogs didn't hit scent. Finally, it flushed from a cedar just a few feet from me. A quick shot followed it into the brush. After Casey fruitlessly hunted "dead" throughout the vicinity, I conceded a miss. Going back to the antlers, I decided it was easier to walk twice as far carrying half as much weight. I walked forward with one antler and the shotgun, then went back for the other two. The process was tedious, but much easier. It took three back-and-forth shuttles to reach Rebel's grave.

I brought an antler and the shotgun beyond the grave to a place where the trail entered an alder thicket. Vivid memories of a hot August evening when I carried another load through that thicket—the limp body of Rebel—washed over me. It was a struggle to put them out of mind. On the second trip, I paused again at the grave. Casey stood beside me. Abby pawed at the hole in the ground. Two grouse for dinner rested in my game bag. Vikki would be tickled with the antlers. The afternoon was a gift that needed acknowledgment.

"Thanks Reb," I said.

A heck of an opener

The truck was loaded and the canoe was on top. It was the first day of duck season and we were going out for the noon opener. I let the dogs off their leads in the back yard and they made an exuberant dash around the house as I walked toward the truck. I waved at my neighbor, who was driving by on the county road in his truck. I hadn't heard him coming, and hoped the dogs didn't run out in the road. Then I heard the awful sounds of pain. Running toward the sound, I saw our yellow Lab, Casey, lying in the road. Abby, our German shepherd, was moving at a trot. Casey tried to stand and fell down.

So much for duck hunting.

My neighbor and I got to Casey about the same time. The dog was conscious, alert, and breathing hard. He'd try to stand and immediately go down.

"I think I ran right over him," my neighbor said. "I never saw them."

We decided to get Casey out of the road. I looked up to find Abby. She was nowhere to be seen and didn't come when I called. My neighbor thought he'd hit her, too. Carefully, we carried Casey over to where my truck was parked and laid him in the grass. Then my neighbor went off to look for Abby while I called Vikki at work and left a message that she should try to find a vet. She called back a few minutes later. Since it was Saturday, the nearest vet services were in Two Harbors—100 miles away. I told her to make the 20-mile drive home from work and secretly hoped Casey would last until she arrived.

Then I started paging through a Thunder Bay, Ontario, phone book.

A call to a medical emergency line connected me with a vet clinic. I told them we'd be there in a little over an hour. Then I called another neighbor who's a paramedic and left a message on his answering machine, asking him to stop by if he could. My last call was to a friend at the Hovland Post Office to put out the word that Abby was missing. I went out to check on Casey. He was lying on his side and panting, but still alert. My neighbor came back—no Abby. There wasn't much to do but wait for Vikki to get home.

"Hang in there, big guy," I told Casey.

A car pulled up. A man I'd never met before got out, introduced himself, and said he'd heard at the Hovland Post Office that Abby was missing. He volunteered to look for her. To make a long story short, Vikki came home. I walked around the yard and nearby woods to look for Abby and, not finding her, decided to hustle Casey to the vet. Our friend the paramedic came over as we were leaving and said he'd look for Abby, too.

The drive to Thunder Bay was high speed and took forever. Vikki sat with Casey in the back of the station wagon. We weren't sure he'd make it to the vet. Time was of the essence. I drove to the head of the line at a road construction site and was allowed go on as soon as the road was clear. Canadian Customs quickly passed us through. We made it to the clinic. The vet said she was optimistic because Casey was clear-eyed and alert, although obviously in lots of pain. For the next three hours, he was the center of attention at the clinic, where he was examined, X-rayed and placed on an IV. He responded to the TLC, and thumped his tail—hairless for several inches at the tip where it was shaved to bandage a nasty split—every time veterinary technician Amy entered the room. Dogs know who their friends are. I called Hovland once from the clinic to see if Abby had been found—no luck. Vikki needed a hug.

Casey's prognosis was better than we expected. It appeared that the truck had run over his chest and shoulders. The X-rays showed some internal bleeding and air leakage from the lungs, but the vet found no broken bones, dislocations, or internal injuries. He was prescribed pain, antibiotic and anti-inflammatory medication—and lots of rest. We were home before dark— no Abby. Vikki drove off to look for her. I answered a telephone call from our paramedic friend, who'd spent three hours in an unsuccessful search. When we hung up, I went outside to begin a search of my own. A frightened, battered Abby was at the back door.

She was struck in the hind quarters. That night, the paramedic came over and stitched up a nasty tear on her leg. A Monday veterinary examination found she was badly bruised, but had no apparent serious injuries. That night, she had spring in her step when we took a short walk.

Remarkably, Casey is able to stand and walk long enough to eat and go outside. He spends most of his day napping—which is nothing new. Hopefully, he'll recover and resume his daily walks in the woods. As for Vikki and me, we're thankful to have our two dogs, because for several hours, we weren't sure if either one would be with us. Casey and Abby are an important part of our household. Any dog owner knows what we mean.

We're also thankful to live where we do. On Saturday afternoon, at least four individuals dropped what they were doing to spend hours looking for Abby. It's hard to express enough gratitude when folks do things like that. We were amazed, too, at the kindness and generosity shown by people along the road to Thunder Bay, at the construction site, at Canadian and U.S. Customs, and at the veterinary clinic. Since Saturday, neighbors and friends have stopped by, called, or e-mailed to wish us well. Some folks may think this is a lot of to-do for a couple of dogs. But as one neighbor told us, dogs are part of your family.

Dad's moose hunt

"Your father must be making the neighbors nervous," Vikki observed when she heard Dad was practicing moose calling in his Duluth back yard.

Dad and Mom drew a coveted Minnesota moose license for a zone near my North Shore home and he was preparing for the hunt. Having heard his calls, I was nervous, too. He didn't sound like a lovesick cow moose. Instead, he sounded like he'd hurt himself. Fortunately, when opening day arrived, my friend Orvis Lunke of Hovland produced a commercial moose call. All you had to do was blow into it to sound like a cow moose. Hopefully, it would sound enticing to a lonesome bull.

Orvis and I were accompanying Dad on his hunt. The hunting rules allow people to tag along with a licensed moose hunter, but not assist in the hunt. The three of us hunt deer together, and we wanted to share in this once-in-a-lifetime hunt. Another member of our deer hunting crew, Alan Lutkevich of Duluth, planned to meet us later in the day, after he'd fished some North Shore rivers for salmon. Actually, Dad had hunted moose once before. Prior to the once-in-a-lifetime rule, four of us drew a tag and I shot the moose. This time Dad was on his own, because commitments kept Mom at home. He wanted a bull, but wasn't concerned about the size of the horns.

"I'm looking for something to eat," he said. "You can't eat the gol-darned horns."

Opening day dawned windy, miserable, and spitting snow. We went to an area where recent logging had left a series of cutover areas. Moose frequent these openings and browse on the abundant new growth. We walked perhaps a half mile without seeing anything. Finally, we reached a turn in the trail where trees blocked the breeze.

"Let's try calling here," Dad said.

A moose call sounds like a dairy cow making a lonesome moo. You call a couple of times and then wait for a bull moose to step out. It works.

"There are two of them," whispered Dad.

Sure enough, two bull moose were ambling up the trail toward us. A young bull with spike antlers was in the lead. Behind him was a larger bull. The small bull stopped and turned broadside.

"Should I shoot him?" Dad asked.

"Shoot the big one!" Orvis and I replied.

A moose that's facing you doesn't present much of a target, even for a high-powered rifle like the .270 Dad was shooting. It's best to shoot at a moose broadside, so you can aim for the vital heart and lungs. The bigger bull was facing us. He stopped, but another call got him ambling up the trail. He walked into a dip, disappearing from Dad's view, because he was sitting down to shoot.

"He's lying down," Dad whispered.

"No. He's still coming," Orvis answered.

"Get on your knees so you can see," I advised.

"Stand up," Orvis advised.

"Keep the gun on him," I suggested.

"I can still shoot the other one," Dad whispered.

"Shoot the big one!" we both answered.

The bigger bull came over a rise in the trail and kept coming, narrowing the distance between us to half a football field.

"Should I shoot?" Dad asked.

"Wait until he turns," Orvis said.

"Keep the gun on him," I said again.

The bull came closer still. Then he turned and stepped into the brush before Dad could pull the trigger. The small bull had disappeared on the other side of the trail. We hustled down to where the moose had been, hoping the bigger bull had paused beside the trail. He hadn't. I heard a crack where the small bull had walked into the alders. Then I heard another crack. And another. Suddenly the alder brush was whipping about. Unseen in the moving brush, the small bull was coming back—and he was headed towards Dad. Now, Dan Perich is a little hard of hearing. He didn't hear the cracks and thrashing brush. And he was walking through a wet area and looking at his feet. So he didn't know a hairy locomotive was headed his way.

We waved. We gestured. Finally, Orvis ran over to him and pointed into the woods. The alders were thick, so the bull was darned near close enough to touch and still out of sight. However, he was now close enough that Dad could hear him and see the waving bushes. Then, when it appeared hand-to-hand combat was imminent (and with Dad, certainly not out of the question,) the moose caught our scent and made a crashing retreat. All and all, it was an intense start to a once-in-a-lifetime hunt.

"How come you guys wanted me to shoot the little one after it ran in the brush, but you didn't want me to shoot it before?" Dad asked.

We didn't answer.

"This is the first time I ever hunted with coaches," Dad mumbled.

Further up the trail we reached a giant clear cut. There were so many moose tracks that the ground was torn up like a Chicago stockyard. But we didn't see any moose. We walked from one end of the clear cut to the other. Then we walked across it. By this time, Dad was starting to lag behind. We climbed a ridge ahead of him—and watched a massive bull high-step it into the brush. Wide, palmated antlers flashed in the sun as the bull walked into a spruce swamp from the edge of the cutting. Our hunter was on the other side of the ridge, looking at his feet. We waved. We gestured. Finally, never noticing, he caught up with us.

The bull was likely standing just inside the trees, but he wouldn't come out for the call. However, a cow stepped out and walked along the edge of the cutting for a distance before going back into the spruces. We thought the bull would follow, but he didn't. That was fine. It was just 9 a.m. on opening day. We began a long circle back to where we'd parked, passing another group of moose hunters at a distance in the clear cut. Since there were only four state licenses for this expansive hunting zone, as well as handful of tribal hunters, we were surprised to see them. When we reached the road, we happened upon their trucks parked about a quarter mile from us. Al was there and we headed out to sneak up on some potholes to celebrate the noon opening of the duck season. Orvis and Dad stuck together. They ate lunch, napped, and went hunting. All along the way, even when Orvis was napping, Dad told stories.

Later, when we met up with them, Dad said, "I was trying to tell him a story and the next thing I know, he's snoring."

Our plan to return to where we saw the big bull the next morning was foiled when the four of us arrived before daybreak to find a truck from the other hunting party already parked beside the trail. We went in anyway, figuring that in their haste to beat us to the big clear cut, these competitive hunters would rush past everything else in this huge area. Tracks in the frost indicated that was exactly what they did. We took our time. It was a cold, still morning. The sound of the call carried like a lonely trumpet. And it was lonely, because Dad had no responses. Once, we came upon very fresh moose tracks in the frost. Dad sneaked into a nearby clear cut with Orvis and called. Orvis could hear the moose, but unfortunately it walked away.

"This group hunting is different," observed Al as we continued on.

It was. The four of us walked quietly along forest trails, talking only in occasional whispers. Inveterate roamers all, we settled into a rhythm. This morning, we'd cover some ground. When we finally paused for a midmorning break, we were within a rifle shot of the Canadian border, in a remote, beautiful valley where flames of fall color rippled up a high ridge that rose above us. Leaves fluttered off the aspens with the slightest breeze. The view alone was worth the walk. We saw more country, but no moose, on a circuitous hike back to the trucks. We paused to rest and eat lunch. Dad put Orvis to sleep again, so he wandered over to my truck and told Al and me stories instead.

We tried calling at a couple of places that afternoon, then headed for another cutting. We sneaked into the clearing, called, and waited. Then Dad motioned to us. A moose was coming. The bull plodded up a skid trail. Dad was standing by himself, so this time there was no whispered advice from his companions. He lifted the gun. The bull came closer. He fired and the moose dropped. A second shot anchored it.

Dad was smiling and shaking hands. At 70, he'd killed his first moose on an outstanding hunt. And the three of us who accompanied him were tickled, too. The knives came out and we went to work. In less than three hours, the bull was skinned, quartered, and back at the truck. Within 24 hours, it was butchered and in the freezer. The young moose had small antlers, but tender meat. Dad now has another story to tell. I've already heard it several times and will likely hear it again. That's fine. The moose hunt was a once-in-a-lifetime experience. But the memories last forever.

One last cast

Heavy frost coated the windshield at daybreak, but a half hour later it was shirt-sleeve warm when I gassed up the truck before crossing the Canadian border. Skies were clear and expected to stay that way. In short, it was a perfect October day to go fishing. My destination was Lake Superior's north coast, where heavy rains filled trout streams with spring-like flows. A fishing friend reluctantly stuck at work had one request.

"Don't torture me with stories when you get home," he said.

Cold winters aside, it's pretty nifty living just south of the border. A two-hour drive can put you a long way into Ontario, turning dream destinations into day trips. My goal for the day was a steelhead, chrome-bright and about five pounds—the entree for the final fresh fish dinner of the open water season. In fall, you may catch any of Lake Superior's trout and salmon species in tributary streams. You never know if the next fish on the line will be a super-charged steelhead, a 15-pound Chinook, or perhaps a brook trout in vivid spawning colors. Sometimes, you'll catch several species in the same pool. Most of the trout and salmon are there to spawn, but the steelhead, a spring spawner, enters autumn rivers to feed and is in prime physical condition. Catching one is exhilarating. Eating it is exquisite.

I pulled into a riverside parking lot early enough to assure a full day of fishing. Pulling on my waders and my fishing jacket, I took an extra-long spinning rod from my truck and headed for the water. River fishing seems deceptively simple, because you can carry everything you need in your pocket. I had some hooks, sinkers, and spawn bags, and a few spoons and spinners, stowed in pocket-sized containers.

The river made a slick, whispering sound as it slipped over a deeply submerged gravel bar. I stuck a hook through the mesh of a spawn sack and cast it slightly upstream, so the sinkers on my line would pull it through the strong current to the bottom. Then my bait would drift along the gravel bar, a prime lie for trout and salmon. The morning's first strike came on the second cast, when a spawn-hungry nuclear submarine powered downstream at the touch of steel, arcing the limber rod and easily peeling line from a reel drag set much too tight. The end came quickly when the hook pulled out, as it invariably does with a tight drag. Strike number two came on the next drift and the unseen fish immediately threw the hook with a head shake.

Strike number three was the dinner fish. A five-pound steelhead, strong and bright, rocketed three feet from the water. The drag was now properly adjusted and didn't hinder the trout as it ran downstream. But dinner wasn't ready to be eaten. After a short battle, the steelhead got away.

Sometimes, even beneath a warm October sun, a fisherman can step beneath the shadow of a cloud of bad luck. My fishing mojo wasn't working. Sum totals for the day were a dozen hookups and a handful of missed strikes. Only three "skipjack" rainbows—foot-long immature steelhead—and two chunky, out-of-season brook trout were landed and immediately released. In late afternoon, the locals came out. An old man walked upstream, casting a heavy spoon. It hit the water with a kerplunk. He carried his gear in a small, very worn satchel.

"Are you catching anything?" he asked.

The reply of "only little ones" was met with an indifferent shrug.

"At least you are catching something, eh?" he said. "It is a fine afternoon to be outside."

In October, daylight dwindles, and the inevitability of winter remains an implicit promise. Already the afternoon was waning. Long shadows crossed the river. I shivered and put on my parka, which had been hung from a nearby tree most of the warm day. I continued casting and thought about the ones that got away. Although fresh fish weren't on the menu, it was hard to be glum. I was taking home another form of sustenance. The memories of such a lovely autumn day would carry me through the long winter.

Late for the flight

In the northwoods, Nature and the Department of Natural Resources leave us little time for duck hunting. Winter always comes before you're ready for it. One night, cold northwest winds start to blow, and the snow they carry doesn't melt when it hits the ground. Morning will bring news of fender benders, power outages, and school closings. Only a damn fool or a duck hunter would take a day like this off to go stand in a swamp. I call the boss at home before going to bed.

By 4:30 a.m., heavy snow lies eight inches deep on the forest road; covering but not cushioning the ruts. Three times I stop to clear windfelled balsams with a bow saw by the glare of my headlights, once pinching the blade and wasting precious pre-dawn time working it free. Why didn't I bring the chain saw? At the boat landing the river is nearly covered with thick slush, save for a narrow channel kept open by the current. Nearby aspens creak in the wind as I load the boat and clamp the outboard to the transom. It's a cold sound.

With dog and decoys onboard, I push off into the slush. The yellow lab is eager, standing on the bow seat like Washington crossing the Delaware. The nasty weather has roused his instincts. Maybe the magic of the northern flight is in his blood. Today all the dallying mallards and loafing bluebills still lingering along Canadian waterways must fly or freeze. This is the last hurrah of the fall waterfowl migration, the finale of the northern flight. We are here to send the last ducks south with a bang.

We chug upstream, navigating by flashlight. The slush runs out where the river opens into the marsh. The snow slackens, and the first hint of dawn is in the sky. It'll take fast work to get set up before shooting time. But a three-bird limit will come easy on a morning like this. What if I get three out of the first flock of bluebills? Should I hold out for a curly-tailed drake mallard? Such thoughts prevail as I toss out decoys in the inlet by the scrub willow point. But you shouldn't count your ducks before shooting them. The swamp is ominously quiet. No foolish ringbills try to pitch into the stools while I'm setting up and nothing flushes from the side channel where I hide the boat. My uneasiness grows when the only ducks to pass the point in the dim light before shooting time are a handful of divers that look too small to shoot and a lone, wary mallard. The Labrador looks uneasy, too.

Dawn comes and the ducks don't. The snow picks up again and visibility drops to a few yards beyond shotgun range. An hour after sunrise a lone hooded merganser hurtles out of the swirling white curtain to land among the decoys. The little drake swims like a prince among the fakes, displaying his fine plumage. Hooded mergansers are birds for the taxidermist, not the table, so he's safe here. Safe, at least, until the Lab decides he's had enough of this insolent intruder and lunges from the blind. The merganser flushes and the dog returns, carrying a decoy and black with loon muck. Did Nash Buckingham or Gordon MacQuarry have days like this?

Somewhere in the snow a flight of geese passes by, their cries carried in the wind. The muck-stained dog turns to the sound, and I hit the call. We talk, but the honkers continue south. In this wind, maybe flying over to pay us a visit was just too much work. A half hour later, what sounds like a single passes behind the blind, but never appears. The unseen geese get my hopes up. Surely, we'll see some ducks. Distant hills fade in and out of sight amid the snow squalls. Coffee cools quickly in the cup. Errant gusts ripple and hiss through the marsh grass and slip beneath my parka like cold fingers, but I'll stay warm while the coffee and granola bars last. The dog's not much for coffee, but he'll stick it out as long as I share my granola bars.

We are not the only hunters in the swamp. Across the channel, something moves against the wind. A red fox leaps atop a muskrat house along the far bank. It sniffs, scratches at the rat's thatched roof and continues up the shore. The fox pauses to investigate every hump and tussock, casting sly glances at the decoys. The dog watches the fox intently. "Stay," I whisper, knowing that he won't. When the fox is directly across from the blind, the Lab makes his move. He hits the water with a splash that sends the fox bounding across the marsh. The dog swims the channel nevertheless, and returns to the blind with another coating of fragrant loon muck. At least he didn't retrieve a decoy this time.

The snow lets up; still no ducks. Occasional ravens, year-round residents of the North, flap across the marsh, undaunted by the weather. Sporadic flocks of songbirds go by, tossing like feathered confetti in the wind. A northern harrier swoops over the decoys and lands in a nearby snag. When I next glance at the snag, the hawk is gone. No migrant tarries on a day like this.

Far up the channel I see a flicker of motion. Hark! Could some ducks be swimming this way? False alarm. Whatever is swimming in the channel has fur and four legs. Beaver? Muskrat? Soon two heads poke up from the water like posts. Otter. They, too, are coming toward the blind. This isn't a duck hunt, it's a Walt Disney outtake. Soon four otters are cavorting in the channel. The snow and the cold have no apparent effect on their playful spirits. They swim with their tails waving above the water and dive so frequently that it is hard to keep track of them. Then all four climb ashore on the far bank and hold a conference about the decoys. They move in unison with a weird undulating motion that almost makes them appear as one four-headed animal. After much gawking, all four swim over to investigate the decoys. They're nearly to the furthest blocks when the dog takes another plunge. All four otters dive and don't resurface until they're a safe distance downstream. This time, the dog is shivering when he returns. The snow picks up again and soon his master is shivering, too. It's time to get the boat and retrieve the decoys. The warmth of the truck will feel awfully good. I unload the gun and duck season is over.

"Well, Old Dog, we missed 'em," I tell the mud-covered Lab.

I feel cheated. This is October, dammit. Can't winter wait? But I know better. I came to the marsh today to say farewell to autumn and discovered it had left with the ducks during the night. Still, it was good to sit in the swamp before freeze-up. Now it is time for the marsh to sleep, snug beneath a blanket of snow and ice. In April, the ducks will come back here—they always do. And next October, so will I.

Deer
Season

Free advice

A friend is joining our hunting party for his first deer hunt. Since announcing his decision to do so several months ago, Dave has been deluged with instructions and advice from the rest of us: the grizzled old-timer, the outdoor writer, and the upstart who's shot three bucks since he began hunting with us three years ago. Dave is a bird hunter, but big game hunting is an entirely new experience. In terms of hunting knowledge, you could say he's a freshman ready to become a sophomore.

His instructors have varied credentials. The old-timer has earned his deer-hunting PhD. The outdoor writer is in graduate school. The upstart is working toward a four-year degree with honors. The old-timer introduced Dave to centerfire rifles at a shooting range. They shot one afternoon until Dave's shoulder was black and blue. The old-timer—who can call shots taken at a running buck with open-sighted Model 94—wasn't satisfied with his performance. He advised Dave to get out with his .22 and to shoot, shoot, and shoot some more. He did, and demonstrated noticeable improvement with deer rifles in a gravel pit last week. He took home the rifle he's borrowing with more advice: practice with an empty gun in the living room, shoulder the rifle, and acquire a sight picture. We hope he's doing that, too.

The outdoor writer gave Dave a tour of the hunting grounds—accompanied by the old-timer and the upstart—and admonished him for devoting only one day to scouting. They walked the country, with Dave duly entering landmarks into a new GPS unit. They looked for scrapes, antler rubs, and deer droppings, finding enough that all were enthused by the end of the hike. The upstart is spending Dave's money on everything from a GPS unit to a grunt call to blaze orange clothing. He is also providing Dave with a topographic map in case the GPS batteries wear out. By the time November 8 rolls around, Dave, like all deer hunters, will be cash-poor and gear-rich.

He's also getting a wealth of free advice. By now, he's heard the old-timer's half-century repertoire of hunting stories at least twice. Who knows how many times he's listened to the upstart's tales of three hunting seasons? Even the outdoor writer has shared a story or two. Of course, this is fun for all concerned and adds immeasurably to the anticipation of the hunt. Rare, maybe nonexistent, is the northwoods deer hunter who doesn't enjoy talking about those magic sixteen days in November. For many of us, the remainder of the year is just time to pass until the next deer season.

Introducing a novice to the sport—whether a kid or, in Dave's case, an adult—helps sharpen that enthusiasm. It also makes a seasoned hunter think about all the skills and lessons learned in the woods. That hunting knowledge is passed along to the novice—as it has been since prehistoric men (the first outdoor writers) painted their hunting stories on cave walls. Still, experience remains the real teacher. No one can tell Dave what a deer sounds like as it quietly approaches. No one can describe how he will feel when a buck steps into view. And no one can explain what it is like to kill an animal large enough to supply you with meat for the winter.

The only way Dave can learn these things is to spend time in the woods—a lot of time. Deer hunting is mostly about patience and accepting Nature on its own terms. Sometimes you get lucky and shoot a buck on opening morning, but that's about as far as luck will take you. More often, you'll earn your deer. If

Dave shoots a buck on the opener, none of us will begrudge his good fortune. We may even help drag it out. More likely, though, Dave'll see some chickadees, be entertained by a red squirrel, marvel at the raven's remarkable vocabulary of croaks, and never fire a shot. That's how deer hunting goes on most days and is what Dave probably expects. We've already explained that northwoods venison doesn't come easy–even when you get a little help from your friends.

Al makes venison

The wolf tracks were fresh in the dusting of predawn snow. It was now fully light and I was sneaking, due to circumstances beyond my immediate control, downwind and following the path of a hunting wolf. This is not the best way to hunt for deer. No matter. I'd just left the truck and would turn to face the wind when I was a little further into the woods. There was plenty of room for the wolf and me to go hunting. My friend, Alan Lutkevich of Duluth, was off in another direction. He was the only human hunter I was likely to encounter in a huge block of national forest land near Grand Marais.

It was Thursday and we were entering the final, four-day stretch of northeastern Minnesota's 16-day firearms deer season. There were no deer on the meat pole. This was a concern, but not a great one. The last four days of deer season are often the best ones. The weather is cold and snowy. Few hunters are out. If you like to roam the woods, these are ideal hunting conditions. Even though the wolf was right ahead of me, I walked slowly and quietly, stopping every few steps to look and listen. At daybreak, deer are on the move. You never know when you might see one or what else you might see. That morning, I saw a red squirrel fall out of a spruce tree. The tumble was unintended, and the squirrel landed with a plop just in front of me and scampered away. I was happy it hadn't landed on my head.

The wolf's walking tracks suddenly became bounds. Apparently it had heard or smelled me. Our paths diverged when I turned to work across the breeze. There was a lot of old deer sign, none fresh. On mornings such as this you pick up the pace, trying to find the deer. This was a fine place for a long, quiet hunt. I crossed swamps, skirted clear cuts, padded through big timber, followed the crest of a high ridge, and dropped into dark ravines. But I saw few fresh tracks and no deer. Around ten o'clock I ended up back on the road, not far from the truck. Facing the wind, I crossed the road and started north. Two rifle shots cracked in the distance, the only ones I'd heard all morning.

North of the road was new ground, so my hunt became an exploration. Soon I found myself at the base of a long hardwood ridge that was criss-crossed with old deer tracks. It was open there and you could see a long way. I started along the east side, going slowly, watching, hoping to intersect with a roving buck. Climbing the ridge, I looked back to see the distant blue of Lake Superior. Perhaps deer were scarce, but the view was terrific. Near the crest of the ridge I found a dark thicket of spruce and balsams. Perhaps a deer was hiding there. If it was, I didn't find it. But I did find a small clearing and a dilapidated log building. I walked around, wondering what had once existed at this place. Had it been a homestead? A logging camp? A glance at my watch cut these musings short. It was time to turn around if I planned to return to the truck by noon.

Al wasn't there when I got back. In the snow were tracks of the heavy plastic toboggan we use to haul deer. This was a surprise. I remembered hearing the two faraway shots. Al must have fired them. I followed the toboggan tracks down a logging road and then through a steep, deep ravine, rock-hopping across the creek at the bottom and climbing up the ridge on the other side until I found a game trail running along the crest of the hill. The sled tracks turned on the trail and a couple of hundred yards down the ridge I came upon Al, huffing his way uphill with an eight-point buck in tow.

"I'm beat," he said.

I handed him my gun and grabbed the tow rope. The sled didn't level the hills or clear the brush and blowdowns. But the way it slid across the rugged ground sure made a hard job easier. Before long we were back to the logging road and I'd heard Al's hunting story. He was sneaking through some conifers and heard a sound behind him. Suddenly, a forkhorn bounded out. Before he could shoot, two other deer appeared—a doe and the eight-point buck. He killed the eight-pointer. Talking about it, we figured the bigger buck was chasing the smaller one from the doe. The deer probably weren't aware that Al was there. Although such moments may be a common occurrence in the deer world, a northwoods hunter is a rare witness. Al happened to be in the right place when all heck broke loose and he made the most of an instant of opportunity.

Hunting whitetails on their terms—sneaking through the woods rather than waiting in ambush on a stand—is a low odds game. Usually, the ever-alert deer will hear, see, or smell you first. You must be quiet and focused, fully a predator, to get the drop on a buck. Generally, you have but a few seconds to see the deer, identify that it has antlers, and shoot. There is no room for error. Move too quickly and the buck will see you and escape. Hesitate for a moment and it may vanish, too. Hunters screw up more often than whitetails do.

I saw fresh "wolf" tracks again on Sunday. This time they were made by my friend Orvis Lunke of Hovland, tracking a buck in falling snow. To make a long story short, Orvis made a circle to try and head off the deer, but he never cut the tracks again. It turns out that the buck, another eight-pointer, had made the fatal mistake of stepping out in front of Al. We are indebted to him for our venison.

Two bucks, too close

Due to fortuitous circumstances, two fine whitetail bucks are presumably still roaming the North Shore hills. Fortuitous, that is, for the deer. Not so fortuitous for me. Vikki called it operator error. Dad called it buck fever. But what do they know? OK, so I had two bucks within...bayonet range. OK, and so both of them got away. It is somewhat painful to tell what happened—our deer hunting crew is aching from laughter. You'd think someone would at least compliment my stealthy skill as a deer stalker. No way. Between jokes they complain that the Perich households will come up short on venison this winter.

The first buck appeared on a morning when the weather was a sloppy mix of wet snow high in the hills and thick rain down near Lake Superior. The snow started sticking to the trees at daybreak. When the temperature warmed at midmorning, wet globs began to melt and fall from the limbs. All you could hear were plops and drips. Occasionally, an overladen branch would break and fall. The deer weren't moving much, but you could sneak silently through the sodden woods. I'd just crested a ridge, watched the hillside below for several minutes, and was starting down a rocky ledge about as wide as your driveway.

Suddenly, I heard a noise behind me. I turned, expecting to

see a falling tree. What I saw was a bounding buck. It appeared to be a 10-pointer, but I wasn't counting tines. Instead I was trying to fit my leather glove into the trigger guard of my rifle. Ever had one of those dreams where you try to run away from some danger, but you're frozen in place? It is very similar to watching a nice buck run by at less than 20 feet while fumbling with your fingers. Without gloves, I would have had plenty of time to get off two point-blank shots with my bolt action rifle. As it was, I finally got my finger on the trigger and pulled up the rifle as the deer leapt down from the ledge. I fired one shot as it disappeared.

Though dumbfounded, I was pretty sure I'd missed. Before following after the buck, I first backtracked and saw from the hoof prints in the snow that he had followed me down the narrow ledge. Why? Perhaps his usually keen senses were hampered by the weather. Happening upon me was a complete surprise for the buck and his dash for safety took him right past me. Twice I looked at the place where I'd stood as the deer ran by. Yup, it was less than 20 feet away.

There was no blood in the tracks when I moved forward, which wasn't a surprise. In fact, the deer jumped from the ledge and then walked away through heavy cover. I followed, quickly and quietly, knowing the forest cover opened up further down the hillside. Maybe I'd get a second chance. This time, my gloves were off. I saw the buck again, but he saw me first. He quickly walked away, disappearing before I could get a shot.

A week later, in similar weather, Buck Number Two got away. Shortly after daybreak, I sneaked into a dense conifer thicket were deer often hang out. Immediately, I came upon the fresh tracks left by a small deer. More whitetails were likely lurking nearby. I paused to wipe water off the lens of my rifle scope so I'd be ready for a shot. Then I pushed, as quietly as possible, through one hundred yards of nearly impenetrable, snow-laden hazel brush.

A small opening in the brush seemed like an oasis, so I paused again. Sometimes, with what seems a sixth sense, you realize intuitively that you are among the deer. Alert and ready,

I trusted that familiar instinct and remained still. Soon I heard a deer walking to my right, just beyond a blowdown that blocked my view. The whitetail wasn't likely to come any closer to me, so I pondered my next move. Then a buck grunted off to my left. Slipping a grunt call from my pocket, I answered him and then questioned the wisdom of doing so. I was surrounded by balsams the size of Christmas trees. Visibility was limited. Immediately, I heard a deer approaching from my left. I never raise my gun or flick off the safety before visually identifying my target, so I waited. A black nose appeared beneath the balsams, followed by a whitetail's head. Was it a doe? The head turned, and a high antler tine appeared. No, it was a buck—a nice one.

As he stepped into an opening in the trees, I lifted the gun. The scope was blurred with water, but I could see the buck and centered the crosshairs on the fatal spot behind his front shoulder. He was turning away, about to disappear. I squeezed an immobile trigger—and realized too late that the safety was on. The buck disappeared before I could flick it to the off position. Dad always says that you hunt whitetails for days to get a few seconds of action. He's right. My opportunity to shoot this deer—at a range of less than 50 feet—was but an instant. And, for the second time, I goofed.

I have killed deer. I will kill deer again. We will not starve this winter. I tell myself these things when, at the oddest times, one or the other of these bucks vividly appears in my mind. Regardless of the outcome, few experiences are as intense as the momentary encounter between hunter and prey. I will long relive the moments when the bucks got away. It is not a bad lot.

Settling In

A hunter's Thanksgiving

Last summer, I got a countertop from a friend who'd remodeled his kitchen and installed it on a workbench in my garage. It's the only flat surface under my control (Vikki rules the kitchen and living room) that remains free of clutter. Stored in a bench drawer are my knives and sharpeners. On a shelf are my cutting boards. Nearby are the old school-desk tops that I use to filet fish and trim cuts of game. When the need arises, my garage becomes a butcher shop.

The shop was first put to use last summer, when the Hovland Volunteer Fire Department was given a road-killed cow moose by the local conservation officer. Ever see one of those documentaries where native people kill a whale and the whole village turns out to cut it up? Hovland works the same way. My neighbor showed up with a Bobcat to hoist the moose from the game warden's truck. In short order, the beast was skinned and quartered. Knives flashed while five guys went to work. Vikki wrapped the steaks. A friend hauled off five-gallon buckets of meat to grind into hamburger. Within a few hours, everyone was heading home with shopping bags of packaged moose meat.

The next morning, my neighbor stopped over to retrieve his Bobcat from my driveway. The moose head was hanging from the upraised bucket on a chain in plain view of the county road. My neighbor and I paused for a moment to take in this strange and gruesome sight.

"We had to let the neighborhood know we scored," he said.

My butcher shop has since been used to process fish, grouse, ducks, pheasants, three deer, and another moose. You never know what's on the menu around here. But you will know that it's been processed with pride. The purpose of hunting is to eat. We put as much effort into preparing and cooking the animals I kill as in any other aspect of the hunt. You can show an animal no greater respect. Many primitive peoples believed that a prey animal offered itself to the hunter. The animal would give its life to sustain the lives of others. Killing, the consummate act of the hunt, was an intensely personal moment between predator and prey. The hunter thanked the animal for its ultimate act of charity.

We still do. On Thanksgiving, we gather at the table to give thanks for the bounty our world provides. At the center of the table is the turkey, a bird that symbolizes the hunt. It is surrounded by the fruits of the garden and the field—mashed potatoes, green beans, and cranberries. The first Thanksgiving was a celebration of survival. The turkeys at the table were killed by hunters. The vegetables were earned through the hard work of the Pilgrims and their native friends.

In those times, your next meal was never taken for granted. People sat down to celebrate the fall harvest knowing that not everyone at the table would survive the coming winter. Before spring arrived, disease and starvation would take its toll. Yet had they gathered in fellowship and gave thanks for what the land provided. Our chances of survival are better today, but we still gather to give thanks. The turkey on the table reminds us that the land sustains us. In the company of others, we celebrate.

A wealth of wood

The other morning I woke to an unfamiliar sound: the hum of our propane furnace. The outside temperature had dropped below zero during the night and our home chilled when the wood furnace burned low, activating the thermostat-controlled propane furnace. Winter had finally arrived. I went downstairs and tossed some split birch into the furnace. Within minutes, warm air was rushing through the ducts. I drank a cup of coffee as the chill retreated, warming up to the day. Welcome, winter. I have plenty of wood.

Stacked outside in three woodsheds are seven cords of dry birch—more than enough to get me through the season. I have a mound of green popple and birch split and curing. A truckload of eight-foot birch is on order. My worldly goods ain't much, but I am wood-rich. Such was not always the case. Two years ago, we moved into this house in November with two cords of birch in the shed. The Mother of All Winters moved into the neighborhood a few days later. By the New Year, the birch was gone—and daytime highs stayed well below zero.

January was spent wallowing through waist-deep snow, hacking down dead popple trees with an ancient chain saw and, when that failed, a Swede saw. Popple burns great, but nearly as fast as you can load it into the furnace. Watching my daily toils, the neighbors were greatly amused. I endured many firewood jokes, but soon discovered that most everyone had a woodless winter in their past. In February, I secured a supply of green birch. It fussed and smoldered on the fire, but kept us warm. By the end of March, the next winter's wood was heaped in the yard. We'd turned the corner.

Last year, we insulated the attic to prevent our hard-earned warmth from escaping. Then I bought a new chain saw to make the tough task of putting up wood a little easier. And we had enough dry birch in the sheds to share some with a woodless friend. When you live in the northwoods, it makes sense to heat with wood rather than buy your winter comfort from Big Oil. But self-sufficiency has a price. If you calculate the time and human energy that goes into putting up a winter woodpile, burning wood is anything but cheap...or easy.

As the winter days gradually grow longer, I'll spend time outdoors every evening, bucking, splitting, and piling next year's firewood. It's a tedious, physical task, but working outdoors sure beats spending your evening at a health club trying to keep a desk-ridden body from turning to mush. There's satisfaction, too, in tossing freshly split sticks on an ever-growing heap; a feeling best likened to watching your garden grow or stacking packages of venison in the freezer. Such are the measures of wealth in the woods.

Beavers bring couple nose to nose

"Some guy says he caught 37 beavers in one day," I mentioned to Vikki while looking at an advertisement in a trapping magazine.

"He must be single," she replied without missing a beat.

Beavers have come between us. Until now, Vikki and I have had a good understanding about my outdoor pursuits. She puts up with time-intensive activities like steelhead fishing and deer hunting. She will transform whatever I bring home from field or stream into a wonderful meal. She even lets me keep leeches and nightcrawlers in the refrigerator.

But she's got a thing about beavers.

The flat-tailed critters entered our lives last spring, when I decided to try trapping. I caught a few, and then a few more. Pretty soon, my "rough-skinned" pelts were accumulating in a friend's freezer. An autumn trapping foray added yet some more. I entered the winter with a pile of frozen rough-skinned pelts to be fleshed, stretched, and dried—and a friend eager to reclaim his freezer space.

Putting up a pelt is a messy, tedious task that hasn't changed much since the era when people used stone scrapers to clean

161

hides. Now we use a fleshing knife—a heavy, dull blade with a handle on each end. Otherwise, the process is the same. The hide is draped over a rounded, tapered piece of wood called a fleshing beam. Wearing a vinyl apron, you press the hide against the beam with your stomach to hold it in place. Then you scrape off the flesh and fat with two-handed, pushing strokes. If the going is good, I can clean a pelt in 15 or 20 minutes. A skilled skinner can do it in just a few minutes.

The clean hide is stretched to dry. My friend lent me several pieces of plywood that have concentric circles traced on them. You lay out the hide, which is round, and match it with the corresponding pattern. Then you tack it in place with nails at the head, tail, and midway along the sides. The hide is tightened like a drum. Following the pattern, you pull the hide and nail it in place, eventually ending up with a circular pelt—fur side facing the board—held taut with nails spaced about every inch around its circumference. If you're lucky, your thumb won't be throbbing from a misplaced hammer stroke.

I can put up two or three beaver pelts during an evening in the garage, listening to the radio with a fire crackling in the woodstove. Each pelt looks a little better than the previous one. The only way to become proficient at putting up fur is through experience. I've been climbing a steep learning curve. My friend showed me how to flesh and stretch beaver on a warm afternoon last fall. Under his guidance it seemed easy enough. However, my first pelts were less than perfect. Some were stretched oblong rather than round. Some had tears in the hide. I forgot to pull up and tack the leg holes, too. My friend wasn't impressed when he reviewed his student's work.

The biggest problem was that I'd missed some spots of fat when scraping the hides, which slowed the drying process. Also, the drying boards were in a cold area. I took hides from the boards without realizing they weren't fully dry, but partially frozen. Some pelts had oily, soft spots.

"You should bring the pelts into the house and dry them near the wood furnace," suggested my friend.

This didn't fly with Vikki. What she really doesn't like about beavers is their odor, a pervasive, sweet scent reminiscent of fresh-cut aspen, their favorite food. Vikki dislikes that smell so much that she makes me shed my fur-processing clothes in the laundry area.

"You stink," she frequently tells me.

Bringing aromatic pelts into the house was out of the question, so I put them by the woodstove in my workshop. That helped, but since I only have a fire in the stove for a few hours each day, the process was slow. In desperation, I brought four pelts with soft spots into the house and put them by the wood furnace while Vikki was at work.

I was in the garage, amid fur, when she came home that evening. She looked in on me, commented on the smell, and went into the house. The expected fireworks did not erupt. I waited a while, then curiosity got the best of me. Walking toward the house, I watched through the window as she sprayed air freshener. The kitchen was rank with the chemical scent of "Spring Bouquet" when I stepped inside.

"I thought one of the dogs was sick," Vikki said by way of greeting. "I went all through the house looking for a mess. Then I recognized the smell. Get those things out of here."

Eventually, she relented and let them stay. It was a pragmatic decision: the sooner the pelts dry, the sooner they'll be shipped to a fur auction house. But Vikki hasn't changed her mind about beavers. And as long as her nose is in working order, she never will.

Chickadee cheer

I can't imagine a winter without chickadees. Flitting, picking, scratching, singing, they attend to the dire business of survival with an air of cheerful enthusiasm. The appearance of chickadees at the bird feeder warms the most bitter winter day. At our house we have two bird feeders and—if a pine marten doesn't steal it—a suet ball. We feed the birds for our sake, not theirs. Thousands of songbirds survive Minnesota winters without the aid of sunflower seeds or suet. We offer the birds a free meal because we enjoy their company.

Bird feeders give us a kitchen window view of the wild world. Every day we're entertained by our regular visitors— acrobatic chickadees, upside-down nuthatches, raucous pine siskins, and belligerent bluejays. Occasionally, we're surprised by strangers. One winter a beautiful silver coyote showed up beneath a feeder, although it was probably more interested in the other dinner guests than any tidbits we had to offer. Once, in late October, a bear that should've been in bed climbed up on the deck and pulled down the feeder hanging from the eave. We found its calling card (a thank you, perhaps?) on the lawn the next morning.

But we don't begrudge the bear its snack, nor the coyote's. Too often, back-yard birdwatchers begin considering some critters good and others villains. Squirrels, for instance, are usually despised as gluttonous bullies. Hawks, owls, foxes and other flesh-eaters are never welcome. Yet the small critters that we feed are destined to become a meal for something else. Outside, around the feeder, a mini-ecosystem functions complete with prey and predators. It's easy to forget that more than a window separates man from this natural world. Chickadees face winter with no more than a few feathers and an insatiable appetite. No wonder so many birds choose to fly south.

However, those that remain are well adapted to the unforgiving climate. Ruffed grouse, for instance, dive into the drifts and roost in snow burrows. Snow is a wonderful insulator, and the grouse are cozy and safe from any predators, save one lucky enough to stumble upon a burrow. In cold weather, grouse spend most of their time beneath the snow, emerging in the evening to feed on buds in the treetops. Then they dive into the snow again. When you happen upon a grouse snug in a snow burrow, it bursts from the drifts with a flurry of wing beats.

Some birds, such as ravens, survive on the wintry misfortunes of other animals. Often, the croaks and squawks of these oversized crows will lead you to the scene of a wolf kill or some other wild drama. There, in the snow, you can read the story of survival. In addition to the wolves and ravens, you'll see the tracks of fox, squirrels, mice, and even chickadees. Nothing goes to waste in the woods. Like a ball of suet, the dead deer sustains life for other residents of the forest.

But the bright song of a chickadee picking at a deer carcass sounds hollow. It's hard to study such a scene and not feel pity for the deer, which died a terrifying, violent death. Minnesota lies on the northern edge of the whitetail's range, and the severity of our winters is often measured in terms of dead deer. Deep snows and cold weather, especially if coupled with a reluctant spring, lead to starvation and massive die-offs in the state's deer herd. This grim situation always triggers an emotional response from the public, and hundreds of individuals haul hay and corn into the woods to feed the deer. Despite their good intentions, thousands of deer die hungry, proving again that man has little influence over nature's plans.

But those of us who feed the birds don't like to think about such things. Instead we sit, snug with our hot coffee and central heating, and watch winter through the window. We rarely pause to consider how a chickadee can look so dapper after spending a below-zero night roosting in the meager shelter of a back-yard spruce tree. In fact, if the chickadee never returns to the feeder, we won't miss it. Others, equally dapper, will undoubtedly take its place. However, if all the chickadees disappeared, winter wouldn't be the same. Despite the snow and cold, these tiny troupers never seem to let this grim season get them down. Watching them at the feeder, you can't help but admire their plucky courage.

And inside the kitchen, winter doesn't seem so bad after all.

A balsam for Christmas

My father sees the forest for its Christmas trees. When you go walking in the woods with him, he's forever pointing them out.

"That one would make a nice Christmas tree," he'll say.

He doesn't intend to cut the tree down. He just has an eye for Christmas trees. For Dad, many trees grow in the woods, but only the balsam fir is worthy of Christmas ornaments. Spruce lose their needles too soon. Norway pines are ugly. Tree-farmed Scotch pines are too commercial. Artificial trees are out of the question.

The other day, I talked to Dad just before he and Mom left for the woods. Snow was in the forecast and they were driving up to my uncle's property to get their tree. It is hard to find a Christmas tree after a storm because all the balsams look beautiful with a mantle of snow. You have to walk up to a tree and shake the snow loose. Invariably, some goes down your neck. Then you stand back to eyeball the tree.

The perfect Christmas tree is symmetrical, with evenly spaced branches. You can look at a lot of trees, walking slowly around them to view every angle, without finding one to bring home. Most are lopsided, with extra growth on the sunny side. Sometimes, close inspection of a well-formed tree reveals two balsams growing tightly together. Other trees have gaping "holes" in their shape from missing limbs.

When I was a kid, we took some long walks looking for Christmas trees. Dad liked to look at a lot of balsams, eventually selecting one that met his holiday standard. He'd cut it down with a few strokes from a sharp saw. Then he would stand the tree in the snow and admire it.

"It's a little big," he'd always say, "but we can cut it some more at home."

An eight-foot balsam isn't heavy, but you have to be careful not to break the frozen needles or branches as you carry it from the woods. If the snow is soft, you can pull it behind you, leaving a Christmas tree "track" in the snow. A better method would be to carry the tree on a toboggan, but we never did.

It always takes some tinkering to get a tree into the house. Sometimes you have to lop off a foot or two from the trunk. Then you may need to trim limbs and knots with a hatchet so the trunk fits in the stand. Once you set it up in the house, you have to adjust the tree to stand straight. Finally, you can clip the top to make room for the star.

Now it is beginning to look and smell a lot like Christmas in the house. The balsam is an aromatic tree. Nothing in the northwoods smells sweeter than a stand of balsams on a warm June evening. The indoor warmth releases that summer scent from the tree. Dad likes to stand back and inhale it.

"That smells good," he'll say.

Everybody has their own traditions for trimming a Christmas tree. My mother has a collection of ornaments, including some very old heirlooms. Her favorite, ancient and elaborate, features a splendid paper cutout of an old man carrying a Christmas tree. She always hangs it front and center.

Christmas isn't about trees, but there is something about bringing a tree into the home that is Christmas. Green and fresh, a gift from the frozen land, we decorate the tree with colorful trimmings, and use it to light the darkest days of December for our celebration of faith. Beneath the tree we gather with family and friends for fellowship and to exchange gifts. We wish each other Merry Christmas—and renew our human spirit.

Books by Shawn Perich

COLLECTED STORIES

Superior Seasons
Life on a northern coast
2003, North Shore Press, $14.95

Join Shawn Perich in the country he loves—along the wild North Shore of Lake Superior. This collection of outdoor stories and thoughtful essays reflect, with humor and passion, the life of a man who is at home in the northwoods.

OUTDOORS

Whitetail Hunting
By Shawn Perich and Michael Furtman
2004, Creative Publishing International, $21.95

Whitetail Hunting is a complete guide to hunting North America's #1 game animal. Concise text and ample illustrations explain everything you need to know about deer, hunting tactics, and proper equipment to become a successful hunter.

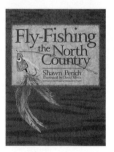

Fly-Fishing the North Country
1995, University of Minnesota Press, $12.95

A unique look at fly-fishing in the northwoods that draws upon the expertise of many accomplished anglers. Advice for catching brook trout, smallmouth bass, northern pike, and other species on a fly. The book includes more than 60 flies designed for fishing northern lakes and streams.

The Northern Ontario Outdoor Guide
With Gord Ellis and James Smedley
1996, The Outdoor News Publications, $8.95

The Northern Ontario Outdoor Guide is a complete information source for planning a fishing or hunting vacation. In addition to a complete listing of resorts, outfitters, and fly-in services, it contains expert advice for fishing, hunting, and travelling in Canada.

Books by Shawn Perich

OUTDOORS

Fishing Lake Superior
A complete guide to stream, shoreline
and open-water angling
1994, University of Minnesota Press, $14.95

A complete guide to fishing Lake Superior and its
tributary streams that presents proven tactics for
catching steelhead, lake trout, salmon, and
walleye. Anglers will find accurate, where-to-go
information for seasonal hotspots and boat accesses.

TRAVEL

The North Shore
A Four-Season Guide to Minnesota's
Favorite Destination
Illustrated by David Minix
1992, University of Minnesota Press, $14.95

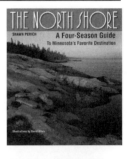

The North Shore is the definitive guide to
Minnesota's wild and beautiful Lake Superior coast.
Using mileposts, the book leads you to parks, water-
falls, hiking trails, villages, historic sites, and vistas.

Backroads of Minnesota
Your Guide to Minnesota's Most Scenic
Backroad Adventures
Photography by Gary Alan Nelson
2002, Voyageur Press, $19.95

A celebration of the state's beauty, Backroads of
Minnesota takes you along driving routes from the
prairies to the northwoods. Stunning photography
by renowned photographer Gary Alan Nelson.

NORTH SHORE PRESS
HOVLAND, MINNESOTA

To order, write or call:
North Shore Press, 5188 North Road, Hovland, MN 55606
(218) 475-2515

Or, visit us online at:
www.northshorepress.com or www.shawnperich.com